GROWING
TREE FRUITS

GROWING TREE FRUITS

Bonham Bazeley

COLLINS

To Phyl, after whom her nurseryman
husband failed to name a plant –
perhaps this book will suffice instead

Frontispiece: Apple 'Lord Lambourne'

Text © Bonham Bazeley 1990

First published in 1990 by
William Collins Sons & Co Ltd
London · Glasgow · Sydney
Auckland · Toronto · Johannesburg

A c.i.p. catalogue record for this book is
available from the British Library

Produced by the Justin Knowles Publishing Group
9 Colleton Crescent, Exeter, Devon EX2 4BY

Editor: Roy Gasson
Line illustrations: David Ashby

Typeset by Keyspools Ltd, Golborne, Lancs

Printed in Portugal by Printer Portuguesa

CONTENTS

FOREWORD

An intriguing question for any thoughtful gardener to ponder in this environmentally conscious age is the role that fruit — and tree fruit in particular — will play in gardens of the future.

The signs are that it could be significant, such have been the developments in the past decade or so that make growing tree fruits in modestly sized gardens a much more attractive proposition. Naturally, more than ever before, the emphasis is on restricted forms of training, the use of rootstocks that will make the best possible use of available garden space in relation to crop yield, and the choice of varieties of high quality that can reasonably be expected to do well in the conditions provided.

As to the satisfactions experienced when fruit is grown to a high degree of excellence, none perhaps is more pure than to have produce pristine fresh from the tree for immediate use, and, if one is a reasonably good planner, for use from store, in the case of apples, pears, and walnuts. (Timing, as Bonham Bazeley explains, is a matter of some importance in picking pear fruits, for they need to ripen fully in store to have the best taste.)

It needs only a little thought and imagination, too, to make well-trained fruit trees into highly decorative garden features, as the author of this excellent book has shown on numerous occasions, most notably in a series of gold-medal gardens staged at the annual Chelsea Flower Show in the 1980s.

Crucial to the heightened profile of fruit growing in gardens, however, has been the work of the plant breeders and horticultural-research stations both here and abroad, and, in equal degree, progressive nurserymen such as Bonham Bazeley, who are the link between them and the gardening public.

In the case of the author of this book, his flair for innovation has led him to test out and introduce various novel forms of training for tree fruits — some new, others adaptations of long-forgotten practices unearthed during his researches into fruit growing long ago.

If I were starting to grow tree fruits now I would wish for no better guide than this book. But its usefulness goes way beyond the needs of the beginner and it will make a valuable aide-mémoire for experienced fruit growers. The author's touch is as sure on historical matters as on the wide selection of varieties he describes, and on the practicalities of tree-fruit growing. It is a notable addition to the literature of fruit growing.

Robert Pearson

INTRODUCTION

Over many years of talking to people with gardens I have found that most of them either know very little about growing tree fruits or, if they do have some knowledge, find it all somewhat confusing. If you fall into either of these categories, I hope that this book will help you to understand tree fruits and so lead on to the wonderful experience of producing and eating fresh fruit from your garden – not only apples, pears, and plums but cherries, figs, peaches, and quinces, even medlars, mulberries, and walnuts.

While commercial orchards and fruit nurseries are usually established on land suitable for the purpose, amateur gardeners have other criteria for choosing where to live – finding the perfect setting for the planting of fruit trees is unlikely to be among them. The hope that the soil will be the 'deep and well-drained friable loam' so beloved of gardening writers, but so seldom found in practice, may also be forlorn. Most of us must make the best of the conditions of climate and soil that we find where we settle – fruit growing, like politics, is for many of us 'the art of the possible'.

My many years as a nurseryman with a special interest in tree fruits and how best these can be grown in home gardens perhaps gives my advice a special flavour. Above all, it is based on realism. I take heart from one of my horticultural heroes, the great nurseryman Thomas Rivers, who wrote in 1871: 'the soil here varies from a light calcareous sand to a stiff loamy clay ... the temperature ranges lower than that of the Horticultural Gardens at Chiswick and the climate is dry.... Pears differ so much in quality with very slight variations of soil and climate that much allowance must be made.' Nevertheless, he was one of the most successful tree-fruit growers of his time.

My history of tree-fruit growing in Britain and the United States of America, brief as it is, shows how painfully slow has been the progress towards making this an easy task for the layman to undertake. But the story also tells how much important work has been done at research institutions since the late 1940s. Both rootstocks and scion wood used in the production of tree fruits are now much healthier, thanks to advances in recent years, and the new dwarf stocks make the planting of apples and plums, in particular, far more of a possibility even in quite small gardens.

It is often said of various aspects of gardening, and it is certainly true of tree-fruit growing, that the chief requirements are a little knowledge and sharp pruning shears. If you can supply the latter, perhaps you will allow me in this book to provide the former.

A History of Fruit
Growing

FRUIT GROWING IN BRITAIN

Since very earliest times the inhabitants of Britain must have varied their diet by eating wild fruits, including, we know, crab apples, cherries, and sloes, but there is no evidence that they cultivated fruit trees before the coming of the Romans. The invaders, though, were keen gardeners and farmers and they enjoyed eating fruits, especially those they had been familiar with in Italy. They imported fruits to augment the locally available food and they probably planted orchards to grow apples, pears, and cherries. They certainly used apples because pips, possibly of cider varieties, have been found at several Roman sites in Britain, notably at Silchester and Bermondsey. They also introduced their favourite vines

Opposite: peach 'Rochester'. Below: an old-style cherry orchard in flower in Kent

from continental Europe, as well as medlars, mulberries, and walnuts, and doubtless they regretted that the British climate was not more suitable for growing other fruits from around the Mediterranean, such as the peach and the apricot.

We know nothing about the story of fruit growing in Britain during the first two centuries or so after the Romans left. But, by the middle of the 7th century, fruit trees were being cultivated in the monasteries, many of which had close connections with continental Europe. The monks gradually introduced new varieties; by the year 1000 they were growing apples, cherries, peaches, pears, quinces, and nuts as well as grapes and herbs. Domesday Book recorded 38 vineyards, in the south and west of England and as far north as the Midlands, by the latter part of the 11th century. The monks also planted cider orchards; two apples recorded in the 13th century were 'Costard' and 'Pearmain', both of which were grown for making into cider as well as for eating.

In the gardens of the wealthy, as well as in monastery grounds, peaches came to be grown, usually with some form of protection, as were quinces for marmalade or for adding to apple pies. Pears, too, became popular for cooking and for making into perry or mixing with ale, new varieties being brought to England from the west coast of France. Some fruit trees must have died out, because in the 13th century fresh imports were made from Italy of medlar, mulberry, and plum trees and, probably, of walnuts and sweet chestnuts. Monks, who had long collected fruits from the countryside, established the practice of selecting the best-fruiting trees and bushes in the wild, transplanting them into the greater protection of their gardens, and then propagating from these improved clones.

It is perhaps not too imaginative to date the beginnings of commercial fruit growing in Britain to the 14th century, when Edward III granted large numbers of new market franchises and made the weekly local market a commonplace of national life. Here the surplus produce of the neighbourhood could readily be sold and monasteries and other landowners soon joined in this new growth industry.

The Black Death, a new and deadly form of plague, that reached England in 1348, provided a savage interruption. So, too, did a second outbreak in 1361–2 and a third in 1369. A series of cold winters, late springs, and droughts also affected all agriculture and horticulture and resulted in an increasing dependence upon imported fruits and vegetables from across the Channel. Nonetheless, the pattern had been set.

Henry VIII was responsible for an upsurge of interest in fruit growing. In 1533 he sent Richard Harris, described as his 'fruiterer', to France and the Low Countries to study fruit growing and to bring back trees and grafts of the best apples, pears, and cherries he could find. Harris then planted a model orchard of about 80 acres (32 hectares) on royal land at Teynham in Kent from which grafting wood was distributed to other growers as far away as Derbyshire, Lancashire, Suffolk, and Gloucestershire. The king also employed John Wolf, a French gardener-priest, to design pleasure gardens for the royal palaces at Whitehall and Hampton Court; Wolf is credited with having introduced to Britain the first apricot trees. Henry also built Nonsuch Palace at Cheam in Surrey, with plenty of garden walls on which to train fruit trees and, just before his death in 1547, bought, for £60, new gardens and orchards at Greenwich.

Among the finds raised in 1982 from Henry's warship *Mary Rose*, which sank off Portsmouth in July 1545, was a basket of well-preserved plum stones. From these, the pomologist Dr Peter Dodd identified five varieties of plum, which must have been harvested just before the ship sailed. One was 'Myrobalan', first recorded by John Gerard in 1597 in his *Herball*; the others were 'Catalonia', 'Green Gage', 'Mirabelle de Nancy', and 'Yellow Cherry', all first recorded in 1629 by John Parkinson in his *Paradisi in Sole Paradisus Terrestris*.

Between 1630 and 1649, the two John Tradescants, father and son, were royal gardeners to Charles I; they travelled widely abroad and collected many plants for growing in England. They popularized the cultivation of apricots, cherries, pears, peaches, plums, nectarines, and quinces in many of the large gardens then being planted in the wake of the king's own horticultural enthusiasm.

In 1664, Britain's Royal Society published the diarist John Evelyn's *Sylva*, a book that long remained the classic guide to tree planting in landscape gardening. This, though, was not the author's intention; his interest lay in meeting a chronic shortage of timber for the navy. Together with *Sylva*, Evelyn issued *Pomona: or an Appendix concerning Fruit-trees in relation to Cider*. In this he explored at length the art of grafting and use of rootstocks, the stocking of apple and pear orchards, and methods of planting, pruning, and fencing. Evelyn later collaborated in the translation from the French of a book called in English *The Compleat Gard'ner*, whose author was a colleague of the great garden designer, André Lenôtre, at Versailles. This work made detailed observations on how best to grow pears, peaches, grapes, melons, and plums.

In 1732 a nurseryman named Robert Furber issued a catalogue of 364 varieties of fruit available from his Kensington nursery; many of these trees would have been imported from abroad and it was a common complaint that nurserymen did not always supply true to name. *The Compleat Gard'ner* had given advice on 'discriminating the several kinds of fruits so as not to be confused and taken in by exotic names bandied about by nurserymen'. Partly because of this difficulty, and that of transporting trees around the country, wealthier landowners started to establish their own orchards and vegetable gardens, surrounded by high walls on which to train fruit trees. The walled gardens, usually established at some distance from the big house, soon began to include heated greenhouses for the choicer fruits and vegetables. Rivalry between landowners to have the most comprehensive collection of fruits led to the raising of rootstocks and the grafting of selected scion wood from trees of proven worth. Gardeners, with under-gardeners to help them, became skilled in the production of fruits and vegetables to provide a continuous year-round supply for the kitchen and dining room.

The loss to Britain of its American colonies had an indirect effect upon fruit growing. Sugar became scarce and expensive and consequently jams and preserves became luxuries. Fruit consumption fell and commercial growers started to grub out orchards, turning to the now more profitable cereal crops. In addition, at about this time, a severe epidemic of canker attacked fruit trees and a new aphid-borne disease, known as American blight although it was imported from France, spread through the nurseries and orchards. These problems hastened a decline in the health and vigour of fruit trees on the bigger orchards and, to add to their problems, growers had to suffer the discomfort of the 'little ice age', when a series of lower-than-usual winter temperatures was recorded.

Early in the 19th century there was a resurgence in fruit growing in England. Much of the credit for this belongs to one exceptional man, Thomas Andrew Knight (1759–1838), a rich landowner who, at his Herefordshire estate, researched into many agricultural and horticultural subjects, including fruit growing. He studied techniques of grafting, the effect of rootstocks on the growth of scions, the ascent of sap and the formation of branches on trees, and the comparative influence of male and female parents on their progeny. He was the first systematic British plant breeder and he produced improved varieties of apple, cherry, damson, nectarine, and pear.

When, in March 1804, a small group of men founded the Horticultural Society of London, it was Knight whom they asked to prepare the paper setting out the society's objectives. Knight pointed out that by then societies for the advancement of most of the arts and sciences had been formed, but that 'horticulture alone appears to have been neglected, and left to the common gardener, who generally pursues the dull routine of his predecessor; and if he deviates from it, rarely possesses a sufficient share of science and information to enable him to deviate with success'. Knight was president of the society from 1811 until his death.

In 1818 he established an experimental garden of $1\frac{1}{2}$ acres (0.6 hectare) at Kensington. The garden was moved in 1821 to a site of 33 acres (13.5 hectares) at Chiswick and here were planted trials of all the known varieties – 3,825 in all – of a wide range of fruits, as well as many vegetables and ornamental plants from all over the world.

This was a period of great fruit-growing activity. Nurseries prospered around London. Many of our classic apples appeared. Fruits could be exhibited at the Horticultural Society's shows (inaugurated in 1833) and receive publicity. New technology and new design made possible more and better greenhouses for raising less hardy subjects. The building of the railways transformed the transport system and enabled produce to be moved more quickly and efficiently around the country; as a result, orchards could be replanted or established in areas that were suited to fruit growing, even if they were not near towns. Soft fruits were often inter-planted between top fruits as jam making began to prosper again.

As the new rich built their big houses with their walled gardens, more and more greenhouses came into use, particularly after the excise duty on glass was abolished in 1845. Many of the new men of property were interested in growing fruits for their tables, often in semi-jocular competition with their neighbours.

To serve these, and other, gardeners there were a large number of flourishing nurseries. Some were newly established, but several had long been in existence. That of Thomas Rivers and Son, for example, had been founded in 1725 at Sawbridgeworth, Hertfordshire, and when Thomas Rivers (1798–1877) succeeded his father in 1827 he became the fifth generation to manage his family firm. From his youth, Rivers had specialized in roses and his firm's catalogue listed probably the finest collection in the country. In 1850, however, he turned his attention to the breeding of fruit trees, inspired by the work of Thomas Andrew Knight. He soon produced 'Rivers' Early Prolific' plum, followed by other plums and gages, nectarines, peaches, and 'Early Rivers' cherry. He also published a number of books and leaflets that became very popular and ran into many editions, notably *The Orchard House* and *The Miniature Garden*. The latter described some of his experiments with root pruning, manures, grafting, rootstocks, and the growing of dwarf fruit trees in pots. His knowledge as a practical pomologist and hybridist meant that his advice was sought far and wide and for over twenty-five years there was scarcely a season when he did not introduce a new fruit variety from Sawbridgeworth.

I have a copy of Thomas Rivers's catalogue dated October 1862. Pears take pride of place at the beginning, with 86 cultivars, plus 30 selected new varieties and 10 recommended for baking and stewing, listed and described – all grafted on both pear and quince rootstocks. Seventy-one 'select apples' follow, with 44 more 'for the kitchen', on crab or paradise stocks. There were 17 apricot cultivars, 42 cherries, 10 figs, 73 grapes, 4 medlars, 19 nectarines, 22 peaches, and 74 plums, all described and priced. Soft-fruit bushes were also listed, with notes on their production and planting hints. Roses were listed in a separate catalogue. It amazes me how Rivers could control the growing of all these fruit trees, mostly in several shapes and ages, and on more than one rootstock, as well as supervise a big collection of roses and an intensive breeding programme of new cultivars, yet still keep the business profitable.

Thomas Rivers was succeeded by his son, Thomas Francis, who continued fruit breeding and introduced the peaches 'Duke of York' and 'Peregrine', more nectarines, and the pears 'Fertility' and 'Conference', all of which are still being grown today. He bred also many other varieties that, although less successful in their own right, were used as parents of later crosses. When Thomas Francis died in 1899, aged 69, he and his father had been very largely responsible for the total number of new fruit trees introduced by their firm – 27 plums and gages, 32 peaches, 21 nectarines, 3 pears, 3 cherries, 4 apples, and an apricot. The nursery was carried on by his descendants until 1985.

Another disciple of Thomas Andrew Knight made his mark as a raiser of new fruit trees and vegetables. This was Thomas Laxton (1830–1893), who trained and practised in the law but gave this up to devote his life entirely to the attempt to ascertain the principles of heredity in plants. Very few people knew the process necessary to obtain definite crosses, by which is meant the removal of the anthers and petals from the selected seed, or female, plant in order to ensure that the only pollen to reach it will be that of the chosen male parent, manually applied. Thomas Laxton knew and practised this long before Mendel's laws were published in English, cross-breeding many garden plants, including strawberries, roses, pelargoniums, and garden peas. He even conducted a number of breeding experiments for Charles Darwin, who was also ignorant of Mendel's theories.

Thomas Laxton was joined by his sons, Edward and William, who started the work of cross-breeding the best cultivars of apples, pears, plums, and soft fruits on a considerable scale. Their work resulted in the introduction of at least seventeen new apples, three pears, and nine plums, in addition to over fifty strawberries and a long list of gooseberries, currants, and roses. As Laxton Brothers of Bedford they made about two hundred crosses a year of trees growing in pots in the big fruit house in which they first raised apples as well known as 'Laxton's Superb', 'Fortune', 'Lord Lambourne', and 'Epicure', as well as others less familiar. 'Laxton's Superb' pear and 'Early Laxton' plum were theirs, too. Later generations of the Laxton family continued to breed and grow fruit trees near Bedford until 1957.

Many of the fruit trees produced by Laxton Brothers and other nurseries were grown in comparatively small quantities for some years after their raising, a slow and costly business. Only gradually did demand for them grow as they became better known, often as the result of publicity gained through articles in gardening magazines and by word of mouth. Horticultural shows, too, at which new varieties could be put before the public, helped to spread knowledge of fruit growing. The first summer show of what was now (since 1861) the Royal Horticultural Society was held in 1888. There were other shows and other societies. Robert Hogg (1818–97) was one of the founders of the British Pomological Society in 1854 and he worked hard to popularize fruit-growing in gardens and the exhibiting of fruits at horticultural shows. He also published several books on fruit growing, including *The Fruit Manual* (1860) and the *Herefordshire Pomona* (1876).

In 1904 the Royal Horticultural Society opened its gardens at Wisley in Surrey, allocating several acres to fruit and the promulgation of proven methods of cultivation and the growing of improved varieties. A year earlier, the first British fruit research station had opened at Long Ashton,

Bristol, its particular interest being in cider apples and fruit-crop nutrition. In 1907 a laboratory was opened at Wisley that, under the direction of Frederick Chittendon (1873–1950), carried out important pioneer work on the self-sterility of fruit trees. East Malling Research Station opened in Kent in 1913 under the direction of Dr Ronald Hatton. In spite of cramped quarters, insufficient land, lack of finance and all the confusion caused by World War I, the range of Malling fruit-tree rootstocks was collected, classified, and tried out, using vegetative methods of propagation, the results being published in 1918 and 1919. Another important development was the establishment in 1909 of the John Innes Horticultural Institution with the acquisition of land at Merton in Surrey. William Bateson, the first director, and Sir Alfred Hall, who succeeded him from 1926 to 1939, both carried out genetic experiments in fruit-tree breeding from which much evolved later.

World War I interrupted commercial tree-fruit growing and after it was over many old orchards were grubbed out and apples were imported from the United States of America to meet the winter demand. British growers had difficulty in producing 'Cox's Orange' apples to compete, largely because of scab disease – although the Seabrook family grew 'Cox's Orange Pippin' trees successfully on their land in Essex where the bright sunshine, low rainfall, and more suitable soil made this variety less susceptible to scab and canker. Another problem was that available methods of spraying were inefficient, even though the first knap-sack sprayers had reached Britain from France in 1891. Finally, the huge decline in the use of horses on the land and for transport cut off the main source of abundant manure, which, on one market garden late in the previous century, had been applied at the rate of 30 tons to the acre (75 tonnes to the hectare). The study of growth-producing substances and selective weedkillers was, although becoming increasingly important, then still in its very early stages.

The National Fruit Trials – jointly sponsored by the Ministry of Agriculture and the Royal Horticultural Society – began in 1922 to build up at Wisley a collection of apples, pears, plums, and cherries, to observe their habits, evaluate the fruit, and sort out the nomenclature. These were the first such trials to be set up anywhere in the world. Research into the long-term storage of apples and pears resulted in the first commercial gas store being opened in 1928 so that British fruit could have a much longer season, thus encouraging growers to plant up more land. Orchards were replanted mostly with 'Cox's Orange Pippin' and 'Bramley's Seedling', often with 'James Grieve' and 'Worcester Pearmain' as pollinators, and with lesser numbers of 'Grenadier', 'Newton Wonder', and the new cultivar 'Laxton's Superb'. Growers were kept informed of advances in the control of pests and diseases and of improvements in the machinery needed to apply the necessary sprays and cultivations. Various methods of planting and pruning were tried out at the research stations and the resulting advice promulgated, first to commercial growers in their trade press and then to amateurs through the increasingly popular gardening magazines.

Times were not altogether easy for fruit nurserymen in the 1930s. I see from my father's old catalogues that three-year-old bush apple trees, grafted on 'selected stocks approved by the Ministry of Agriculture', were being offered at only 3s 6d (17½p, 85 cents) each. Then, during World War II, fruit trees became scarce on nurseries and development slowed down once more as land was given over to corn crops and orchards deteriorated. By 1946, the best bush apple trees available were selling at 15s (75p, $3) each, but quality had necessarily slipped and a long haul back had to begin.

Because of the need to replace imports from the United States in order to conserve dollars, British fruit growers were encouraged after the war to replant their land with the best cultivars. In 1947 the Ministry of Agriculture took over the entire responsibility for the National Fruit Trials and planted up a new field on high ground at Wisley with the most extensive collection in Britain of all types of hardy fruit. The Royal Horticultural Society then made a group of model fruit gardens to demonstrate how a wide range of fruit can be grown in a private garden where space is limited. The National Fruit Trials were moved in 1952 to new land at Brogdale Farm, near Faversham, Kent, where the National Fruit Variety Collections are still held. These contain approximately 2,000 apples (probably the most comprehensive collection anywhere in the world), 500 pears, 350 plums, and 225 cherries. The purpose of the orchard collections is to provide gene banks for plant breeders, maintain a living reference library of correct nomenclature (there were, for instance, 67 synonyms of 'Blenheim Orange'), and to conserve old cultivars.

An important development for the propagation of fruit trees came when the John Innes Institution co-operated with the East Malling Research Station to introduce the Malling-Merton series of rootstocks, which had a bred-in resistance to woolly aphids (American blight). Of these, MM.106 is still the principal rootstock for semi-dwarfing apple trees and MM.111 that for more vigorous trees. While this work was going on, other scientists at East Malling were using 'Cox's Orange Pippin' and 'Worcester Pearmain' as principal varieties in a breeding programme designed to increase the range of commercial apples, both for the early market and for cold-storing through the winter. Meanwhile, at the John Innes Institution they continued breeding disease resistance into their new cultivars of apple and cherry.

The 1950s and 1960s may have been exciting times in the research institutions, but they were frustrating years on fruit nurseries. Advances seemed to take so long to work through to the gardener-customer. Fresh stool beds had to be planted with the new rootstocks and it took a few years before they became sufficiently established for young plants to be pulled off for lining out and subsequent grafting. For the provision of grafting and budding wood, mother-tree plantations had also to be established on leading nurseries. Consequently, new cultivars were slow to become available for garden planting and catalogues continued to offer the well-tried old names. Meanwhile, commercial orchards were being planted with fewer varieties in bigger numbers in order to provide for the requirements of the new supermarkets and to try and compete with the flood of imported 'Golden Delicious' apples.

In the 1960s, East Malling and Long Ashton Research Stations collaborated in experimental work that resulted in the eradication of various virus infections both in rootstocks and in the principal tree fruits, particularly the more popular cultivars of apple, pear, plum, and cherry. There are believed to be fifteen or more viruses that affect fruit trees in different ways, some by diminishing the crop or suppressing growth and others by blemishing fruit or foliage. By the middle 1970s the research stations were able to distribute virus-free rootstocks, to which their EMLA label was attached, and also fresh, virus-free supplies of all the

Apple 'Suntan' growing at the Institute of Horticultural Research, East Malling, Kent

most-wanted fruit cultivars. The latter were used to replant the mother-tree orchards on leading fruit nurseries so that from then on all grafting wood, as well as the rootstocks, could be virus-free. In this way the health and cropping capability of young trees leaving nurseries has been considerably improved – probably the greatest advance in fruit growing to date.

Simultaneously with these research programmes, lengthy trials have resulted in new cultivars of apple, pear, and cherry being released first to commercial orchards and then to amateur growers. Examples are the apples 'Greensleeves', 'Jupiter', 'Jester', 'Redsleeves', and 'Bountiful', now being followed by 'Fiesta' and 'Falstaff', and the pear 'Concorde', all bred at the Institute of Horticultural Research, East Malling (to give it its new title), and the cherries 'Merchant' and 'Mermat', bred at the John Innes Horticultural Institution. Many of these have been bred to provide naturally compact trees, with great cropping potential early in their lives, that need far less pruning than older cultivars.

With these and other virus-free fruits grown on the appropriate rootstocks in the healthy EMLA range, the amateur grower now has the opportunity, as never before in the history of fruit growing, of harvesting worthwhile crops from the garden, even when space is limited. And this is only the beginning. The new Ballerina, or columnar, apples have started to arrive, as have genetically dwarfed apple, peach, and nectarine trees, products of horticulturally minded scientists who are able to manipulate the genes of plants to the advantage of the home gardener.

FRUIT GROWING IN NORTH AMERICA

The original Indian inhabitants of North America had few fruits in their diet other than sweet wild plums, which they made into prunes, wild grapes for wine, and various berries, including mulberries, which were found from New England southward to the Gulf. The Spaniards, who came to West Texas, New Mexico, and Arizona in the 16th century, introduced the Indians to peaches, some of which later escaped to the wild, to be called 'Indian peaches'. Jesuit fathers taught the Indians to grow apples from seed, the fruit having been introduced by other settlers, missionaries, and explorers.

Colonists who sailed for America from Europe in the 17th century often took fruit seeds with them. The settlers who founded the Massachusetts Bay colony in 1630 sowed apple seeds from England and, some ten years later, were sampling 'very fair pippins' from the orchard of their first governor, John Winthrop. Most apples were probably more suited for making into cider in those early days and a pioneer Connecticut nurseryman, Henry Wolcott, booked orders for five hundred or more cider-apple trees in the late 1640s.

Many European fruits introduced by 17th-century settlers failed because they could not adapt to the wide-ranging conditions of heat and cold they met in their new homes. Until seedlings from these imported varieties, or from crosses between them, could be grown and tried, reliable American fruits could not be originated. This process took many years. However, some fruit trees planted in the early years were successful and long-lived. Thomas Prence, governor of Plymouth colony, Massachusetts, planted on Cape Cod in about 1640 a pear that lived to the mid-19th century, when it was still producing 15 bushels (550 litres) a year of russet fruits called 'Fall Pears'. 'Warden' and 'Black Worcester', both famous old English pears, lived fruitful lives for just as long.

John Winthrop planted a garden on Conant's Island in Boston harbour, which was glowingly described in 1630 as containing cherries, plums, mulberries, and walnuts, besides a vineyard. He exchanged plants with John Endecott, who alternated with him as deputy and governor and also dealt, before 1641, with George Fenwick of Saybrook, Connecticut, who was probably the first nurseryman in New England. However, for nearly two hundred years the opportunity to domesticate the wild fruits found in America and improve those imported from Europe was largely neglected. The dawn of plant breeding did not really break until the very end of the 18th century, when seedling trees bearing superior fruits were perpetuated by grafting. After the end of the War of Independence, in 1783, Prince's Nursery at Flushing, Long Island, founded 46 years earlier, started to distribute some of these improved varieties; among the plums was 'Imperial Gage', which, renamed 'Denniston's Superb', is still grown in Britain.

It seems that far fewer pear than apple seedlings were tried in North America before Independence, but in the first half of the 19th century new pears from French and Belgian raisers reached the United States. Kenricks of Newton, Massachusetts, for instance, imported from Belgium scions of the still-popular 'Beurré Bosc' pear, which joined 'Tyson' and 'Seckel', both raised in America, and 'Bartlett' from England, as the pears most popular with growers in Massachusetts and the estates along the Hudson River between about 1825 and 1870. During this period growing from seed lost favour as grafting wood of proven varieties became available. Fruit growing was now attracting wealthy patrons, such as William Coxe of Burlington, New Jersey, and Robert Manning of Salem, Massachusetts; both were eminent pomologists and writers who corresponded and exchanged fruits with like-minded men in England, France, and Belgium.

Iowa's first nurseryman was Henderson Lewelling, whose orchard contained 35 varieties of apple as well as other fruit trees. In 1847 Lewelling drove a wagon loaded with fruit trees and good planting soil over to Oregon. Here he met William Meek, who helped him and his brothers Seph and John to start planting orchards and nurseries there; later they expanded into Washington and California.

The American Pomological Society was founded in 1852, to compare and evaluate fruits from all sources, resolve the synonyms by which so many were known, and disseminate information among horticulturists. The first president was Marshall P. Wilder, who personally tested many hundreds of fruit varieties in Massachusetts and did valuable work on nomenclature. Choosing worthy varieties from the thousands of seedling trees being grown was for many years the first priority of the society, particularly at meetings and fruit shows. Fruits were being tried in almost every county of every state, in widely differing climates and soils, and a still-fledgling fruit-growing industry was being kept informed of developments.

In 1873 the society established in honour of their president the Wilder Medal, which was awarded to individuals and institutions whose work had furthered the cause of fruit growing and, even more sparingly, to fruits deemed to be of particular importance. Up until 1939 just twenty-five fruits were so honoured, and only three more to 1970. The first recipient, in 1873, was 'Clapp's Favourite' pear; apples that have won the award include 'Golden Delicious' in 1919, 'Cortland' in 1923, 'Starking' in 1926, and 'Delicious' (in the form of the 'Richard' clone) in 1951.

The United States Department of Agriculture was established in 1862 but it was not until 1886 that a Division of Pomology was included in order to expand work on fruit crops, particularly oranges and grapes. By 1894 Department of Agriculture researchers were beginning to recognize, although by no means fully understand, virus problems. They were studying fireblight in pears and, in 1895, brought to the attention of growers the need for cross-pollination of pears. Their work on figs had direct commercial benefits. 'Smyrna' figs were quite widely planted in California by 1880 but growers were finding it difficult to get the fruits to set. The reason was that this variety is male-sterile. Researchers from the Department of Agriculture found that in Asia 'Capri' fig trees were used as pollinators for 'Smyrna' and imported some trees to test whether they would be similarly successful in the United States. The experiment was a failure, until the researchers realized that the transfer of pollen from 'Capri' to 'Smyrna' depends upon the peculiar life style of the fig wasp (*Blastophaga psenes*) and that the problem would be solved by the wasp's introduction. The promulgation of this information by the Department of Agriculture in 1900 saved the fig industry.

The completion, in 1869, of the American transcontinental railroad made it possible for fruit grown on the west coast to be sold all over the continent and thousands of acres of fruit orchards were planted in the Pacific coastal states. These were the lands where the Spaniards had, between 1769 and 1823, established a score or so of missions where they grew, among other crops, oranges, olives, and dates. This was the area that was eventually to contain the great centres of American fruit growing.

Fruits from Siberia, China, and Japan as well as from Europe all made their contributions to fruit growing in America. Although many of these imports were unsuccessful, some of their seedlings or crosses proved to be

Pear 'Doyenné du Comice'

hardy stock. Siberian breeding stock was imported after the governments of the United States and of Canada sent a joint mission of pomologists to the Imperial Botanic Gardens at St Petersburg in 1882, as part of a search for new and hardier fruit varieties for the many parts of both countries that were unsuitable for existing fruit trees because of low temperatures in winter and short growing seasons in summer. One discovery that resulted was the Siberian crab apple – its fruits were small and only fit for jelly making but its seedlings were entirely hardy. It was used as a seed parent, with pollen from imported European apples. This programme produced new varieties, such as 'Alberta' and 'Columbia', with fruits up to twelve times bigger. Patient experimental crossing and re-crossing yielded more varieties, such as 'Ontario' and 'Crimson Beauty', which are still grown in Canada, even as far north as 58°.

Peter Gideon was an early pioneer who worked for over thirty years, from 1871 as superintendent of the fruit experiment station attached to the University of Minnesota, to produce varieties of apple, peach, plum, and cherry good enough to withstand the severe weather experienced in the Upper Mississippi Valley. He had to complain, shortly before his death in 1899, that really only one good apple, 'Wealthy', had resulted from all his effort. Such is the time scale in which early fruit breeders had to work.

California, too, created, in 1873, its Agricultural Experiment Station. Drainage, fertilizers, viticulture, and wine making were soon being studied and an experimental orchard planted to test imported varieties and provide grafting wood. Other experiment stations have contributed to the great advances made this century in the study of fruit-tree breeding and growing. Those in Idaho, Michigan, and New York have played important roles, as has that attached to Washington University. Great contributions have been made over the years by Summerland Experiment Station in British Columbia, Canada. The new patent laws available to these stations and to fruit-tree nurseries are now helping to compensate them for the heavy costs of raising, testing, and introducing new cultivars.

I have been able in this brief survey to mention only a few of the chief milestones along the fruit-growing road in North America. The work of many scientists at government-sponsored experiment stations has speeded up progress in recent years, but the part played by those earlier keen amateurs who raised worthy seedlings, or noticed 'sports' on their trees, must not be under-rated.

PLANTING AND FEEDING

Previous page: the blossom of apple 'Bramley's Seedling'. Above: apple trees trained over overlapping arches leading to the apple tunnel at Cranborne Manor, Dorset

The planting season for fruit trees grown in the open ground and supplied bare-root (albeit wrapped) begins in late October, when the leaves have dropped and dormancy has begun. It lasts until the middle of April, when the leaves appear again. Frosty weather does not mean the end of the planting season; in autumn frost usually comes out of the ground by the afternoon each day and planting need be delayed only when the ground is too hard for the spade or too sticky following heavy rain. Some trees that have small enough root systems to be contained in pots and have been grown in them for a year or so, such as figs or apples on M.27 rootstock, can be planted from August round to May, so long as they can be watered frequently until well established.

Fruit trees are best ordered in summer, when the new annual catalogues appear from nurseries specializing in fruit trees. You then have time to discuss the fruits, the cultivars, and the rootstocks that will suit you best and also ensure getting your first choices reserved for delivery or collection in autumn. If possible, after studying the catalogues, visit the nursery and talk to someone trained in fruit growing. If you buy from a garden centre, the range offered may be smaller and probably all pot-grown; for the bigger fruit trees this can be very restricting to the roots, particularly if the trees are left in the pots too long. Should the ground intended for fruit trees lie wet and heavy in winter, it would be as well to look to the drainage well ahead of planting time.

On receipt of your fruit trees unpack them out of the wind and soak the roots before covering them tightly to prevent the fibrous root-hairs from drying out while awaiting planting. Remove the top of the wrapping to let air in to the branches. Pot-grown trees can be watered and stood out of the wind until you are ready, with further waterings to prevent drying out. If the planting site is not prepared or you cannot plant within a few days you should heel-in bare-root trees temporarily. This involves opening up a shallow trench in a spare piece of ground, perhaps in the vegetable plot or under a hedge, and covering the roots with fine soil, firming down with your heel.

Prepare to plant by marking exactly where the trees are to go, allowing for the space the fully-grown tree will need. The hole should be dug wider than the spread of the roots and the topsoil put to one side, removing stones, weeds, and any lumps of clay or inhospitable soil that come up. The lower spit, below where the tree's roots will lie, is then forked over and any clay or subsoil removed and replaced by turf, compost, or rotted manure, worked in to provide humus and a free root run. If you are not planting right away, refill the hole with topsoil to save it from getting wet or frosted unnecessarily.

When ready to plant make sure you have good, friable topsoil at hand, mixed about 50-50 with peat and with a little bonemeal added. Try the roots in the hole for size and make sure the tree will be left at the correct depth, with the nursery soil-mark on the stem at soil level again and the graft well clear of the ground. If a stake is required this is driven in next (on no account put the stake in position after planting is completed for this can do much damage to the roots). Place it behind the stem of the tree, making sure that it will not rub a branch.

The tree can be tied loosely to the stake to hold it upright while the planting mixture is worked under and around the roots. Shake the tree as you fill in. Tread the roots down firmly, adding more topsoil until the correct level is reached. Fix the tie to the stake, add a permanent label to a stout branch, and give the roots a good watering to settle the soil around them and get them making new rootlets to grow out into your soil. A tree guard will protect the stem from cats, dogs, rabbits, and mowing machines. This is often the ideal moment to do the winter prune.

A pot-grown tree is planted in the same way except that before placing it in the hole the polythene is slit off and the lower roots are teased out at the bottom to help them make close contact with the topsoil and peat planting mixture. Any weeds around the top of the pot can be removed before the plant is treaded down and more topsoil added. Watering is then very necessary to get the roots growing away from the restrictions of the pot and into your soil, so that the tree may become re-established as quickly as possible.

Roots are all-important. The roots you bought with your fruit tree made

Ballerina, or columnar, apple trees

it grow in the nursery and are now its anchorage; new little root-hairs must quickly grow out from these and start absorbing moisture and nutrients from your soil. Roots cannot function properly if loosened in the soil by the rocking of the tree, which is why staking is often necessary for fruit trees. While the roots are still very small, in the early months of their first season in your garden, they may need your help in dry weather with regular doses of life-giving water.

The soil surrounding the newly planted fruit tree should be kept free of grass and weeds that would compete with it for the available moisture in the early years. Roots of fruit trees planted against walls also have the amount of rain that reaches them somewhat reduced by the foundations and the barrier above them, a point worth remembering in spring and early summer.

Feeding is a subject closely allied to both roots and soil, because shortages of soil nutrients taken in by the roots can upset development. The balance can be corrected by applications of artificial (inorganic) fertilizers such as sulphate of ammonia (high in nitrogen), sulphate of potash (for potassium), or superphosphate (for phosphorus). For instance, if too much nitrogen or hard pruning has led to excessive growth at the expense of fruit buds, it can be controlled by grassing down over the roots to reduce the intake of nitrogen or by applying a potash fertilizer. Nitrogen (N) promotes growth, phosphorus (P) promotes root development and general health, and potassium (K) helps flowers to form and fruit to ripen and also increases resistance to disease. The application of a compound fertilizer can supply a balanced dressing of seven per cent each of N, P, and K to sustain your soil each spring if its balance seems about right.

Concentrated organic fertilizers have the advantage over farmyard manure that they can be bought by mail order for delivery to your door and are a lot easier to handle. Farmyard manure is low in nutrients and can bring in weeds, but it is valuable when well-rotted as a mulch in summer to aid moisture retention, particularly on light or shallow soils, as an alternative to compost or peat. However you feed your trees, remember that the feeding roots that are ready and able to receive sustenance are those at the extremity of the root system and not those against the stem. The outer spread of the branches above ground reflects the position of these roots below.

Most fruit trees prefer a slightly acid soil, that is, one that registers around 6.5 pH when measured with a soil-testing kit. It is often said that plums like lime and it may be right to incorporate this in winter over their roots if the soil is very acid. Fruits that are growing in very alkaline soil having a pH higher than 7, however, may suffer from lime-induced chlorosis; this is shown by a yellowing of the leaves between the veins and the antidote is iron or manganese in soluble form, obtainable from garden shops. Lime does help 'flocculate' or break up heavy clay soil and it contributes to fertility by providing calcium, especially on sour or sandy soils, but it is best to make sure by testing first. It is easier to put down lime than to get rid of it.

Weed control is important under fruit trees because weeds can compete with the roots for moisture and nutrients. They also create damp conditions around the stem, which encourages fungal diseases and offers a hiding place for slugs, mice, or insects. A light forking or hoeing without disturbing the roots is perhaps the quickest way to remove weeds.

PRUNING AND TRAINING

The reasons for pruning can be summarized as follows: 1. To form the strong framework that the tree will need; 2. To induce fruiting, stimulate growth, and control size; 3. To thin out unwanted wood and let in sun and air; 4. To cut away dead, diseased, damaged, or dying wood. Put even more simply, pruning removes wood from where it is not wanted and encourages growth where it is wanted.

To make sense of pruning, it helps to remember the changes that take place in a fruit tree during the growing season. An apple tree, for instance, goes through four modes during the year. Firstly, it flowers in spring, like other members of the genus *Malus*, hoping to attract insects to transfer pollen from its male sex organs to those female ones ready to receive it on another tree. Secondly, it produces leaves (its food factories), new shoots to carry them, and buds for future growth and flower. Thirdly, usually in late July and August, growth slows down and new wood ripens – the tree's main energies are devoted to swelling and ripening its fruit. Fourthly, as autumn turns to winter, the tree drops its leaves and goes into a state of dormancy until the following spring.

PRUNING NEW APPLE AND PEAR TREES

When bush or half-standard trees received from a nursery in autumn or winter are planted, the branches need shortening by about a third. This is to encourage strong new wood from vigorous buds half way down the shoots, rather than from weak ones near the tips; it also reduces the size of the head that the roots must support during the first summer after transplanting. In order to make nearly every bud work for you, either by producing new growth or by making flower buds that hopefully will form into fruit, it is usually sufficient to keep 6–8 in (15–20 cm) of the previous year's growth. In the early years you have to form the framework that will bear all the weight of the branches and the fruit for many years to come. Although the young trees may well have fruit buds on them when they arrive, transplanting may upset fruiting in the first summer.

SUMMER PRUNING OF APPLE AND PEAR TREES

Usually done in late July and August as growth slows down and the tree is changing its priorities from growing to fruiting, summer pruning consists of cutting back the current year's growth on all laterals just above the sixth leaf from the base, ignoring the leaf cluster at the base itself. Leave the leaders alone until the winter prune. This summer prune lets in sun and air to the remaining buds and concentrates food there; fruit is able to ripen more easily and the formation of fruit buds is encouraged.

Opposite: three -year-old cordon apples growing on rootstock M.9 – 'Jupiter' to the right and 'Norfolk Royal Russet' to the left

WINTER PRUNING OF APPLE AND PEAR TREES

When all the leaves have dropped and the tree is dormant the winter prune is done; the shoots already shortened in summer to the sixth leaf are further pruned to three buds from the base and the leader, or continuation shoot, of each branch has between a half and a third of the season's growth removed, leaving the top bud outward-pointing. Overcrowded and inward-crossing shoots are cut right out and thin shoots pruned to short spurs of one or two buds only. Suckers that may have arisen from below the graft must be pulled or cut right out. Winter pruning encourages growth in the following year.

TRAINING OF CORDON APPLE, PEAR, AND PLUM TREES

A cordon tree consists of a single stem from which laterals, or side shoots, have been encouraged to grow out. If the tree is planted at an angle of 45 degrees, rather than upright, its vigour is reduced and more fruiting wood is placed within your reach. Ideally, the rows of trees should be arranged north-south to get sun on both sides, with the grafting union of each tree uppermost. The trees are spaced 2 ft 6 in (75 cm) apart and tied to bamboo canes that are themselves firmly tied to three or four horizontal wires stretched between posts standing 6 ft (1.8 m) out of the ground. These make very useful and decorative divisions in a garden, or black metal frames can be bought for this purpose.

Cordon apples can be grown on M.27, M.9, M.26, or MM.106 rootstocks, pears on Quince A or C, and plums on Pixy only. New growths from side spurs of cordon apple and pear trees are summer and winter pruned as already described, but the leader is left alone until winter, when it is shortened by a third, leaving about 6–8 in (15–20 cm) of new growth. Both processes are repeated each year and in this way high quality fruit is obtained in a small space. Because plum wood should not be cut in the dormant period, pruning of plums is confined to spring and summer.

STARTING WITH MAIDEN TREES

Maiden fruit trees have had one growing season after being grafted on the selected rootstock. They are ready to be trained to whatever shape of tree is required – bush, pyramid, spindle, cordon, fan, espalier, step-over, half-standard, or standard. Starting off with these young trees is becoming much more popular as interest in fruit growing increases, partly because of the greater amount of information that is available on how to train them and partly because of the saving in cost compared with older, ready-trained trees.

Cordon apples growing at the Royal Horticultural Society Garden, Wisley, Surrey

To train up cordon apples and pears from maidens choose trees on rootstocks MM.106 or M.26 for semi-dwarf apples, on M.9 or M.27 for dwarf apples, and on Quince A or C for pears. The leader is cut in winter at about 2 ft (60 cm) above ground in order to check sap flow and encourage side growths for pruning to spurs later; the following summer a new leader is grown on and side growths summer pruned to encourage new fruit buds to form.

To train up bush apples and pears from maidens choose trees on rootstocks MM.106 or M.26 for semi-dwarf apples, on M.9 or M.27 for dwarf apples, and on Quince A or C for pears. The trees are pruned in winter to a strong bud about 2 ft (60 cm) above ground. Three or four branches should grow out next summer to form the head, and from then the advice given for 2-year trees should be followed. When pruning an open-centre bush tree I like to think of each main branch as a cordon and treat it accordingly.

To train up half-standard and standard apples and pears from maidens choose trees on MM.106 rootstock for apples (or MM.111 for weak-growing cultivars and for taller-stemmed standard trees) and St Julien A for pears. Heavily 'feathered' maidens should have two-thirds of these side-shoots removed altogether; the rest, which should be evenly spaced around the stem, are left on but reduced in length by a half. These will help swell the stem and provide extra leaves to supply the tree's 'food factory'. Some cultivars, like 'Bramley's Seedling', make few feathers but any there are should be shortened by a half.

A half-standard apple tree in blossom

Next, you decide what height of stem you require between ground level and first branch; about 3 ft 6 in (1 m) is usual for a half-standard and 5–6 ft (1.5–1.8 m) for a   standard. (Standard pears really need a stronger rootstock than St Julien but because of the length of time they take to come into bearing they are rarely planted in gardens now.) The leader is then grown up a stake or strong bamboo cane until its tip is about 2 ft (60 cm) above the stem height chosen, side shoots being rubbed off; this may take one or two years, depending on the soil conditions and the vigour of the cultivar. Having reached this, the leader is pruned in the next winter, just above a bud about 1 ft (30 cm) higher than the stem height required. The top buds left on the stem will thus be energized to grow out side branches in the following summer and form the framework or head above it. Side growths up the stem can be pruned off to let all future energy go into the head.

OTHER TREE SHAPES

The spindlebush has become very popular in orchards but is less well-known in gardens. It consists of a cone-shaped tree with a central stem, grown against an 8 ft (2.5 m) pole for support, and with wide branch angles. To ensure this, the main side branches are tied down almost horizontally in the early years by means of a string looped onto the branch and tied to a tent peg in the ground. This makes them more fruitful and less vigorous and also allows in more light and air to encourage fruit early in the life of the tree. The upper branches are kept shorter to maintain the cone shape and are pruned to prevent them becoming too dominant or overcrowded. These upper branches are expendable, one of them being periodically pruned back to near its base for a replacement shoot to form. To prevent too strong a leader this, too, is pruned to 6 in (15 cm) or so in winter, the top bud being grown from alternate sides each year and the height being limited to about the top of the pole. The diameter of trees is kept to about 6 ft (1.8 m). For apples, the rootstocks used are M.9 or M.26, or even M.27 for the more vigorous triploids; for pears, Quince A or C. Plums are more suitable for pyramids or cordons on Pixy.

The dwarf pyramid is like a free-standing vertical cordon but with the lower branches allowed to grow out gradually to form a circle about 4 ft (1.2 m) in diameter. The tree normally needs no support and retains its central leader. Only about 6 in (15 cm) of growth is kept each year, the top bud being grown from alternate sides, and the height is limited to about 7 ft (2.1 m). Lateral shoots are best pruned to a downward-pointing bud to help keep the middle open. Suitable rootstocks for apples are M.27, M.9, M.26, and MM.106 and for pears Quince A or C.

Plums can be grown as pyramids on St Julien A rootstock or on Pixy and are best started as maidens. With plums, the maiden tree is pruned back to 4–5 ft (1.2–1.5 m) and branches below 1 ft 6 in (45 cm) are removed after planting. In the first summer branch leaders are shortened to about 8 in (20 cm), leaving the end bud downward-pointing, and laterals to 6 in (15 cm). In the following years the leader is reduced by two-thirds each April until the tree reaches 9 ft (2.75 m) on St Julien A or 6–7 ft (1.8–2.1 m) on Pixy, when the tree is kept at that height. In late July or early August each year branch leaders are shortened to 8 in (20 cm) and laterals to 6 in (15 cm), leaving the end bud a downward-pointing one.

Espalier-trained trees get their name from the Italian word 'spalliera', meaning a supporting piece; they are an alternative to cordons for planting on horizontal wires between posts or against walls. Apples and pears are both suitable for this shape, but plums and the other stone fruits are better trained as fans on walls because they do not respond to the hard pruning required for espaliers. These are usually supplied from fruit nurseries with two horizontal tiers and a central leader off which further tiers can be grown if required. Single-tier espaliers, or 'step-over' trees, when grafted on M.27 rootstock, are very suitable for planting alongside a path next to the vegetable garden; spaced 5 ft (1.5 m) apart they make a fruitful and unusual edging, colourful in blossom and taking very little space, yielding perhaps a couple of dozen apples a year.

Suitable rootstocks for apples are M.27, M.9, M.26, and MM.106 and for pears Quince A or C. If starting with maidens it is best to use galvanized 16-gauge wires, spaced about 15 in (40 cm) apart, stretched between supporting posts placed at 12 ft (3.6 m) intervals. The maiden tree

Opposite, top: a three-tier espalier-trained apple tree. Opposite, bottom: a step-over espalier apple tree growing alongside a vegetable-garden path. Above: an espalier-trained pear tree growing against a wall

is planted 6 ft (1.8 m) from the end post and 6 in (15 cm) in front of the wires. The stem is then pruned leaving three buds just above the lowest wire, the middle one to be a new leader and the others to be allowed to grow horizontally on either side.

In the first summer the new leader is trained vertically up a cane attached to the wires and the two shoots from the other buds are trained on canes at 45 degrees to the wires. The reason for this is that if one shoot grows faster than the other it can be lowered to slow it down and the weaker one raised to speed it up. Both shoots are then lowered to the horizontal in November and tied to the wire. Other shoots from the main stem are pruned to short spurs and any below the first wire are removed cleanly. This process is repeated each year to form new tiers up to the level of the top wire, when the leader is pruned off. In the second and subsequent years shoots longer than 9 in (22.5 cm) arising from the two horizontals are pruned in summer to three leaves above each basal cluster and new shoots from existing spurs are shortened to one leaf above their basal cluster.

Fan-trained trees are intended to be planted against walls in order to benefit from reflected warmth and to make fruitful use of vertical features

Well-grown fan-trained fruit trees at the Royal Horticultural Society Garden, Wisley, Surrey:
above, apple and, below, cherry 'Morello'

of suitable size. Favourably sunny walls are ideal for apricots, greengages, nectarines, and peaches and, of course, for apples, cherries, pears, and plums – although these are normally perfectly productive in the open.

You can buy ready-trained trees or you may prefer to start with maidens and train them to your walls yourself; the method is much the same for all fans, except that stone fruits should be pruned only in summer, preferably when the buds are bursting in spring, in order to minimize the risk of disease entering. They each need a wall width of about 15 ft (4.5 m) and a minimum height of 6 ft (1.8 m). Horizontal wires are fixed at intervals of about 18 in (45 cm) and bamboo canes are tied to these, radiating outwards in the shape of a fan from the stem of the tree.

If starting fan-training with a maiden tree this is pruned back to two stout buds, one each side, about 1 ft (30 cm) above ground; a feathered tree may already have a pair of branches at this height, in which case they are retained but shortened to about 18 in (45 cm). As growth proceeds the following summer the object is to get three or four good 'ribs' to form on each side, leaving the centre fairly open; these should be evident by July when, on each side, one will be extending the leader, two will be chosen to grow upwards and one downwards. Thus, four shoots each side can be trained outwards and the others pinched back to one leaf. Cherries make fewer side shoots than the other stone fruits but should still produce three good ones to form the fan, as above.

Double U-type cordons, their tops grafted together, with oblique cordons behind

S-type, or 'arcure', cordons

Other tree forms can add considerable interest around a garden. Cordons, for instance, can be trained with two branches arising from the stem instead of one; this is a U-type cordon. The branches may even be doubled up again, to form a double U-type cordon, perhaps having each pair of stems bent inwards at the top wire and grafted together.

Another variation on cordon training is the 'arcure' method, in which the main stem, initially planted at 45 degrees, is bent over in a half-circle and next year a branch on the top of the curve is bent the opposite way in similar fashion. Three or four such hoops rise one above the other on a wire fence, each covered in fruit buds all along its length.

A tree looking like a crowned goblet can be formed by planting a strong maiden and pruning the stem at about 2 ft (60 cm) up; four branches can be trained outwards at right-angles towards four outward-sloping uprights. They are then trained up these like cordons and hooped over the top to meet in the centre, side shoots being taken horizontally at two or more levels. A knot can be formed at the top by tying the shoots together in a simple graft.

A variation on the step-over espaliers I have mentioned is the single horizontal cordon. A maiden tree is bent over horizontally and trained along a wire about 1 ft (30 cm) above the ground, toward the next one planted about 3 ft (90 cm) away, making a useful edging. Another

Above: apple trees trained as goblets in the vegetable garden at Barnsley House, Gloucestershire. Below: apple 'Michaelmas Red' trained as a flat-top tree

Apple trees trained into a boat shape

alternative to the single-tier step-over tree is to prune off the leader of a two-tier espalier and confine the tree to these two horizontal tiers alongside a path; you cannot step over this height easily but of course you get more fruit.

A 'flat-top' tree is a shape I have formed with a 'James Grieve' apple on M.27 dwarf rootstock, planted in a tub. Four or more branches from close together on the stem are trained outwards horizontally on bamboo canes to form the spokes of a wheel of about 2 ft (60 cm) in diameter, well-spurred with flowers and fruit clusters, and fun to have on a patio near the house in summer.

Another ambitious form of training is known as boat-shaped and consists of a line of U-type cordons planted parallel to each other, the stems looking like the keel and the branches the ribs of a boat. Wires run the length of the 'boat' and are held at each end by a wooden frame; the whole looks good and makes a most unusual feature growing in a bed cut in a lawn.

FAMILY TREES

These are offered by many nurseries, both on dwarfing and semi-dwarfing rootstocks, and they consist of several cultivars of apple or of pear, carefully chosen to be of approximately equal vigour and to be effective cross-pollinators, grafted on one tree, either bush or fan-trained. In this way one tree in a small garden can do the work of three; or it can even be planted in a tub and taken with you if you move house. The branches should come clearly marked with coloured tapes to identify the varieties for correct treatment, pruning being the same as described for bushes. They need a little more watching than trees with only one cultivar but a good guide for keeping the vigour equal is for a strong-growing shoot to be pruned fairly hard in summer and only lightly in winter, while a weak shoot is pruned hard in winter and not at all in summer.

FESTOONING

Festooning is the bending of the branches to maximize fruiting and limit excess growth; it can be practised on two-year-old or older trees. It is easier with long whippy branches than with short ones. I have found it of particular benefit to plums on the dwarf rootstock Pixy and to apples on the dwarf M.27. Fruit is produced earlier in the life of the tree and in a smaller space than was previously possible, even in tubs.

If a maiden tree is pruned back after planting, as for a bush or half-standard, several branches will grow out the next summer and these can be festooned in early autumn by being tied down and thus helped to form fruit buds. Some side shoots may also form and these can be shortened to make more fruiting spurs or a few may be left for bending the following year; by then growth will be less vigorous and the tree well supplied with fruit spurs. In the case of an older, over-vigorous tree with a lot of unfruitful branches, some of these can be bent down in summer and secured to the stem or even to an opposite festooned branch. Fruit buds form along the bent branches and the top of the tree also feels the check and comes into better bearing.

UNPRODUCTIVE TREES

Some old trees may have been grafted on out-dated rootstocks that have encouraged excessive growth at the expense of fruit, or perhaps faulty or over-zealous pruning has produced the same result. It may be that a judicious thinning in winter, rather than pruning, is what the tree needs. Another cause could well be the over-generous application of nitrogenous fertilizers, in which case grassing over the roots might help. On trees that are not too old it may be sufficient to prune only very lightly in winter and to do so more severely in summer. But if these do not appear to be the reasons for the lack of productivity there are two ancient, but more drastic, techniques which are worth trying in order to check excessive vigour and induce formation of fruit buds.

Root-pruning consists of digging a trench in winter to encircle the tree, some 5 ft (1.5 m) away from the stem. The trench need be no more than one spade's width across. The tree's thick roots are cut through as they are exposed, leaving all the thin fibrous roots intact. This is a treatment that should be reserved for older trees.

Bark-ringing is easier to carry out, but is suitable only for apple and pear trees. It consists of removing a nearly complete circle of bark, $\frac{1}{4}$ in (6 mm) wide, from the stem, leaving at least 1 in (2.5 cm) uncut for sap to rise through. The cuts are made with a sharp knife through the bark and the soft tissue to the hardwood below; this layer is then peeled off and protective adhesive tape, wider than the ring, is stuck over it, bridging the gap but not touching the bared surface. This job is done in spring at blossom time and the tape is removed in autumn when the wound should have calloused over. The effect is to interrupt the downward movement of foodstuffs to the roots, checking growth and at the same time inducing a better fruit set.

Notching, or the removal of a small piece of bark just above a dormant bud, will energize it into growth by arresting the sap flow beyond it.

Opposite: the fruits of an unnamed cooking apple, on a tree grafted by an amateur gardener

BUDDING AND GRAFTING

Keen gardeners who wish to propagate their own fruit trees can buy suitable rootstocks from some specialist nurseries. They will also need a very sharp knife – which should be treated with some respect – and polythene budding tape for tying-in.

T-BUDDING

This should be done when the bark of the stock lifts easily in July or August. The bud-stick must be of the current summer's growth, bearing mature, healthy, plump buds and the stick should be of about pencil thickness, just a little less than the size of stock at budding height. Cut off the leaves on the bud-stick, leaving about $\frac{1}{4}$ in (6 mm) of petiole (stalk) beyond the bud for use as a handle.

Select a straight section of neck on the stock at the chosen height, well above ground level, preferably on the shady side. Make a horizontal cut – the top of the T – around one-third of the stock's circumference, using the middle of the blade and rocking it to penetrate the bark.

Make a vertical cut about $1\frac{1}{2}$ in (4 cm) long downward from the horizontal cut, with just sufficient pressure to cut through the bark. Gently lift back the flaps at the top of the vertical cut to ease the bark clear of the wood.

Hold the bud-stick with the growing tip toward you and select a bud where the wood has started to harden and turn brown, ignoring the top few on the stick, which are probably too green and pliable. Cut below the base of the first suitable bud and slice upward towards you, making a cut not so shallow that you damage the 'eye' of the bud, nor so deep that you get into hard wood. Cut to a position just above the bud, grip the bark between thumb and blade, and pull off this 'tail'. With practice you can cut a shallow sliver, leaving the 'eye' intact and with no need to remove the thin wooden strip behind it; but if the cut has gone deeper than this the strip must be removed by gently bending the tail away so that the wood is detached from the bark.

Holding the bud by the leaf stalk insert it downward into the slit on the stock and under the bark flaps. Stop when the bud shield reaches the bottom of the cut and trim the tail with a horizontal cut, leaving it flush with the horizontal cut on the rootstock. The petiole can be shortened to just over the bud.

Using about 8 in (20 cm) of polythene budding tape make several turns below the bud, jamming one end beneath the second turn, and several more above it, ensuring that the cut surfaces are covered, and secure the end with a half-hitch.

The bud should have 'taken' in about a month and if the stock swells after budding so that the tie restricts growth it can be slit at the back to allow normal expansion. If the budding fails and a dead bud results, you have a second chance without wasting a growing season because you can graft the same stock, just below where you budded it, in the following March.

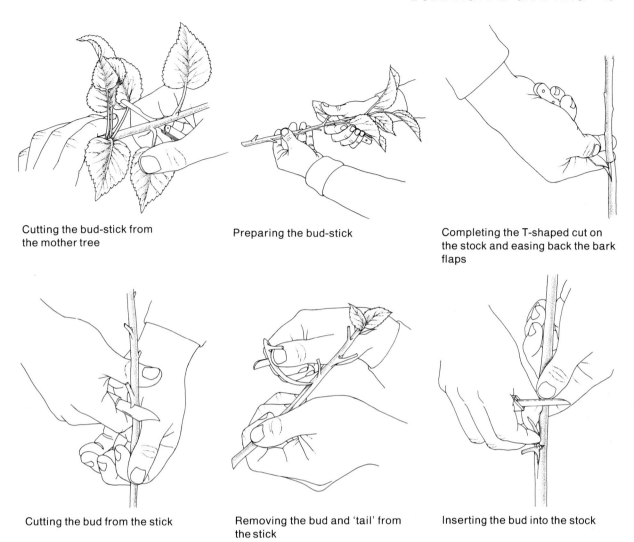

Cutting the bud-stick from the mother tree

Preparing the bud-stick

Completing the T-shaped cut on the stock and easing back the bark flaps

Cutting the bud from the stick

Removing the bud and 'tail' from the stick

Inserting the bud into the stock

CHIP BUDDING

This is a modern alternative to T-budding that professional growers have found to be quicker and more efficient – some varieties of apple and pear that had a high failure rate when T-budded on to certain rootstocks now produce with chip budding a much higher percentage of 'takes'. The bud-stick is prepared in the same way as for T-budding except that the petiole is cut closer to the bud, not being required as a handle. The stock is budded at the same height as it is for T-budding.

A straight section of neck is selected on the stock at the required height above ground level and, holding the knife sideways, a shallow cut is made downward at an angle of 20 or 30 degrees to the stem of the stock.

Keeping the knife at the same angle, another cut is made about $1\frac{1}{2}$ in (4 cm) higher up the stem and directly above the first cut; firstly inward and then downward in one movement to meet it. The knife has to be controlled carefully; it must go no lower than the first cut.

The bud-stick is held with the base towards your body and an area is selected similar in thickness to the already cut area on the rootstock. A cut is made about $\frac{3}{4}$ in (20 mm) below the bud at an angle of 20 or 30 degrees and at the same depth as on the stock. The knife is removed and a second cut is made $1\frac{1}{2}$ in (40 mm) higher up the bud-stick, first inward and then downward to meet the first cut.

The chip with its bud is removed from the bud-stick using thumb and knife blade and inserted in the cut on the stock so that the acute angle of the lip holds it in place. If the chip does not match exactly the cut on the stock, check that the margin is equal on both sides; the top of the chip should not overlap the rootstock bark. If a trim is necessary to match up, cut the rootstock, not the chip.

Tying is done in the same way as for T-budding, using a length of polythene budding tape, ensuring that the bottom cut is well covered. Remove the tape when the stem is seen to be swelling after a month or so.

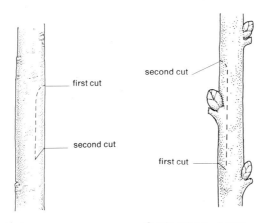

Cutting the stock

Cutting the bud-stick

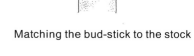

Matching the bud-stick to the stock

Taping the inserted bud-stick to the stock

WHIP AND TONGUE GRAFTING

Whip and tongue grafting is the surest method for amateurs to use, particularly as it can offer a second chance should there be failures following budding during the previous summer. Grafting is carried out in dry weather in early spring, just as the sap begins to rise on the rootstock. The grafting wood should, however, be cut from the mother tree in winter while it is still dormant and stored in the ground or in a domestic refrigerator, wrapped in polythene. There are some occasions when only grafting, and not budding, is possible; for instance, when joining two cordons together at the top of a fruit tunnel after both leaders have grown up to overlap, or when an old tree is being grafted over to a new variety.

The graft, or scion, should have three buds. A sloping cut of 45 degrees is made $\frac{1}{4}$ in (6 mm) above the top bud and a straight, 90-degree cut made $\frac{3}{4}$ in (20 mm) below the bottom bud. These cuts make it easier to distinguish top from bottom and also ensure that rain runs off the top of the scion when in position.

The rootstock is prepared for grafting by being cut down to 6 in (15 cm) above ground level. A sharp knife is then used to make a sloping cut across it, matching in length and area that of the scion to be joined to it.

A knife cut is made across the scion, starting $\frac{3}{4}$ in (20 mm) above and behind the lower bud and ending the same distance below it, in a single, steady, heel-to-toe movement to produce a flat, smooth surface similar to that on the stock.

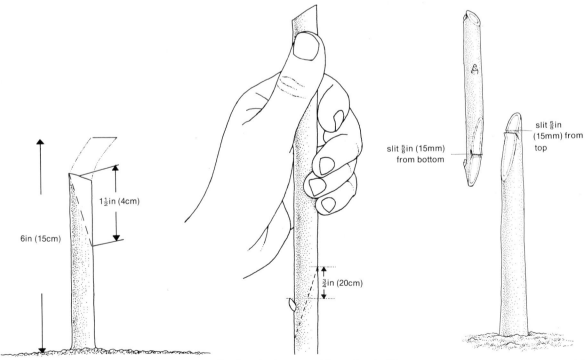

$1\frac{1}{2}$in (4cm)

6in (15cm)

$\frac{3}{4}$in (20cm)

slit $\frac{5}{8}$in (15mm) from bottom

slit $\frac{5}{8}$in (15mm) from top

Cutting the rootstock

Cutting the bottom of the scion to fit the stock

Tongued scion ready to marry with tongued stock

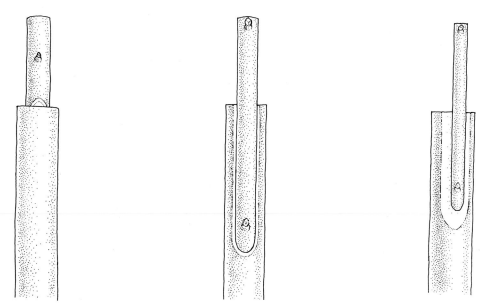

Rear view – the scion should protrude slightly, about ⅛in (3mm), above the top of the stock, producing a 'church-window' effect

Ideal match – the scion is fractionally smaller than the stock

When the rootstock is larger, place the scion to one side, not centrally

Cut a tongue at a slight angle across the scion and, placing it over the prepared stock, make a similar tongue there, an exact match and a tight fit. If the scion is smaller than the stock move it to one side to align the cambium layers, rather than leaving it centrally placed. (The cambium is a continuous layer on the inside of the bark where union takes place first.)

To secure the graft a length of polythene tape is wound around, starting at the bottom and working upward, applying tension without stretching it unduly and keeping the tape flat. Finish with a tie at the back of the stock using two half-hitches. To prevent entry of disease or water into the graft apply grafting wax all over the union, especially between the scion and the top of the stock. To prevent inadvertent knocking of the graft and birds alighting on it, place a bamboo cane alongside.

PESTS, DISEASES, AND
OTHER PROBLEMS

Previous page: silver leaf on a 'Victoria' plum tree. Above: woolly aphids, 'American blight', on an apple branch

There are quite a lot of pests that can attack fruits and a number of diseases or other problems to which fruit trees can succumb. You are most unlikely to meet them all, although practically certain to meet some of them. Most problems can be cured quite easily once you have recognized them and taken the appropriate action. Many can be prevented, for instance by starting with healthy trees from a reputable source. Correct spacing prevents overcrowding and allows for movement of air around the plants and for sun to reach them. Simple hygiene, such as clearing away for prompt burning all prunings and dead wood removed from the trees before they can spread infection, may well save trouble later. By inspecting your trees regularly, particularly in spring and summer, when nature provides a plentiful supply of grubs and insects, partly as food for the rapidly increasing bird population, you can often get early warning of an attack by caterpillars or aphids and rub them out before they multiply, without the need for sprays.

I describe below, in alphabetical order, the pests, diseases and problems that you might come across.

Ants damage fruit trees in two ways: firstly, they eat the fruits of wall-trained apricots, nectarines, peaches, pears, and plums, usually after the skin has first been pierced by a bird or wasp. Secondly, they 'milk' aphids of their honeydew, even herding and encouraging them much as humans do to cows. It is best to put down ant powder on the ground beneath the tree.

Aphids, often called 'blight', affect most fruit trees and come in several colours – green, grey, black, brown, and yellow. The presence of ants (see

Dieback on a peach tree, following bacterial canker

above) may indicate their arrival, or the appearance on the leaves of the sticky honeydew that they excrete. There may be curling of the leaves or distortion of the shoots, while on plums a black sooty mould forms on the undersides of the leaves, which drip honeydew. Woolly aphids, or 'American blight', form colonies on twigs or branches and cover themselves in a white, wax-like 'wool', somewhat difficult to deal with; I find that the best way is to brush them off into a tin of paraffin or petrol. Aphids are sap suckers but they prefer their diet to be slow-moving, so they often land on trees that are not thriving too well, disregarding the more vigorous trees with strong growth. They breed at a fantastic rate, young being born even after their mothers have been killed, thus preventing contact sprays from finishing the job at one application. Systemic sprays applied all over the foliage work through the system, being taken up by the aphids in the sap they suck, soon killing the whole infestation. Aphids should be dealt with when noticed, or even before they attack if a systemic spray is used, as this can last three weeks or so; they are unwelcome because they carry viruses (see pages 65–6), quite apart from reducing the efficiency of the plant's foliage. Aphids do have natural predators such as birds, ladybirds, and their larvae and these can work for you. The traditional remedy of spraying with soapy water blocks the body holes through which the aphids breathe but has to be applied frequently to catch succeeding generations. A tar-oil winter wash can help a lot by killing the over-wintering eggs, but it also kills useful insects.

Bacterial canker attacks plums, cherries, and stone fruits generally, often invading through wounds on the bark, even the scars left by roughly torn-off leaf stalks. The first sign can be on the leaves – brown spots that turn into holes, causing premature leaf fall – or on the branches – shallow hollows that exude gum. There is no positive remedy and trees often recover from attacks, usually thereafter becoming immune. There are sensible precautions to take, such as being careful not to damage the bark in any way, either with mowers or ties, and by pruning only during the summer months and never in the dormant period. If control is attempted, the tree can be drenched with Bordeaux mixture in mid-August, early in September, and again in October just before leaf fall.

Bird damage to an apple

Birds and wasps. Birds are helpful when they eat caterpillars, slugs, aphids, and other pests but a nuisance when they peck out fruit buds in late winter and ripening fruits in summer. It often happens that wasps follow them after the harder surface skin has been pierced. How hard you fight to keep them away will depend on how much you wish to co-exist with other forms of nature. Blackbirds, finches, pigeons, tits, and thrushes are probably the worst offenders and only netting is totally effective against them; this is more easily applied over wall-trained trees. Cotton strands over branches and a distasteful, milk-like spray called Morkit that deters birds are alternatives to various forms of bird-scarers.

Wasps fly out from nests which, if found, can be destroyed; advice can be sought from your chemist or garden shop about wasp poison. Or wasp traps baited with beer can be effective in reducing the strength of attacks when placed near your precious fruit as it ripens. If you tie little polythene bags around your prize fruits to keep off birds and wasps, remember to cut a slit at the bottom to let out moisture from condensation.

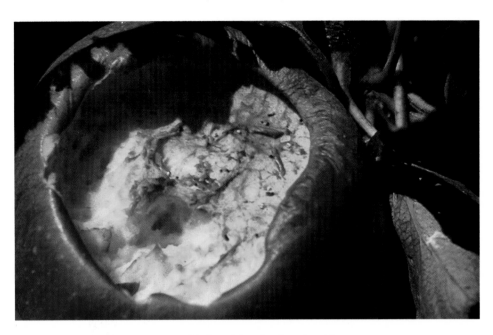

Wasp damage to an apple, after a bird peck has broken the skin

Bitter pit is a disorder that can affect the fruit of certain varieties of apple, either when still on the tree or when in storage. Sunken pits on the surface of the skin with browning of the flesh beneath can often be cut out by peeling the skin, but in severe cases it goes deeper and tastes bitter. It is caused by a deficiency in the release of calcium from the soil, noticed more often on young, strongly growing trees that are overfed with nitrogenous fertilizers. Bitter pit is not at all common but seems to appear in drought conditions and is worse in seasons when there are wide fluctuations of rainfall and temperature. I have had 'Egremont Russet' apples affected and understand that commercial growers of this cultivar look out for the problem. If you suspect bitter pit, take a sample apple to a garden centre or fruit nursery for advice on treatment.

Blossom wilt, when a flowering shoot or truss suddenly turns brown and collapses, is caused by a brown rot fungus that mainly affects cherries but sometimes other tree fruits. A winter wash is a good preventive as part of a standard routine, but there is nothing to be done at the time wilt is noticed, other than pruning it away. The removal of diseased fruit as soon as it is seen is the best form of prevention.

Brown rot can affect all tree fruits but mostly apples, pears, and plums; fruits display a brown decay with whitish pustules of mould growth. It sometimes starts at the point of damage caused by a bird or insect or by bruising caused by bumping against other fruits or branches. The disease spreads very rapidly by contact with other fruits so it is important to inspect trees frequently and remove at once any fruits showing the rot. There is no other worthwhile treatment.

A plum tree affected by brown rot

Canker is different from bacterial canker of stone fruits (see above); it affects most tree fruits but more often apples and pears and other related garden trees and is caused by a wind-borne fungus invading natural openings, scab lesions, or scars left by fallen leaf stalks and pruning. Sunken lesions appear on branches or main stems, surrounded by cracked or corky bark, and extending each year until they surround the stem; this then dies beyond that point as sap can no longer flow through. Small cankered branches must be pruned away and burnt at once, while larger ones can have affected wood scraped away with a sharp knife, the parings being collected carefully, and the wound painted with fungicidal paint. Canker is more likely on heavy soils where drainage is poor, so it is important to attend to this before planting. It is also sensible to prevent rubbing between crossing branches, and between a stem and its stake, as damaged bark facilitates entry of the fungus. Over-generous use of nitrogenous manures, farmyard and chicken particularly, can also increase the susceptibility of young trees to canker and scab. The routine treatment where the disease is suspected is to spray with a systematic fungicide, as advised by a garden retailer.

Capsid bugs are elusive pests visible in May as busy green insects about $\frac{1}{8}$ in (3 mm) long on or under leaves; in summer they are yellow and twice as big. They suck sap from the leaves, puncturing brown-edged holes and distorting the leaves in the process from toxins in their saliva. Damage to the fruitlets of apples and pears leaves typical bumps, depressions, and corky pimples on the surfaces. Tar-oil winter wash to kill eggs in crevices

Canker, that has led to dieback, on an apple branch

of the bark is the first treatment to prevent hatching in about mid-April. A routine spray with a systemic insecticide in the spring, applied according to the maker's instructions, will also control winter moth caterpillars.

Caterpillars, the larval stage of butterflies and moths, arrive in various shapes and sizes but perhaps the commonest and most damaging are those of the winter moth and of the codling, sawfly, and tortrix moths, all described below.

An apple damaged by capsid bugs

Codling moth larvae are the number-one apple pests; they have eight pairs of legs and burrow into the fruit through the eye to feed near the core, only to be discovered when you bite into the fruit or when it starts to rot prematurely or drop off. This problem is best tackled by spraying just after petal fall, again when fruits are the size of peas, and again about ten days later. Caterpillars over-winter in their home-spun cocoons in cracks in the bark or beneath tree-ties and can be killed by the winter wash. They pupate in May and winged moths emerge in the next few

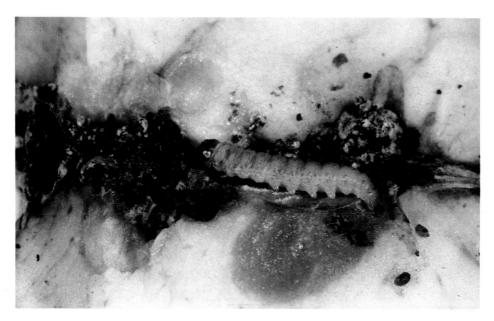

The larva of the codling moth in an apple

weeks to lay their eggs near the fruitlets, evading grease bands, the grubs hatching two weeks later. An alternative control is to hang pheromone traps among your fruit trees to catch the male moths before they breed.

Coral spot fungus affects all woody plants and is recognized as pink pimples the size of big pinheads covering the bark of twigs and branches, which later die back. Prunings and sawn-off branches left lying about or used as pea-sticks can soon become the host to these colourful fungi. The answer is to burn such prunings as soon as made and certainly before the spores on affected wood can be released to enter cuts or crevices on living wood. If coral spot appears on stakes or fences that cannot be burnt then they must be treated with creosote or copper-sulphate solution. It goes without saying that any affected branch on a living tree must be removed neatly and at once for burning since there is no other remedy.

Dieback of young shoots, for no obvious reason, is more likely on the stone fruits than on apples and pears and fairly common on peaches, nectarines, and apricots. I find the most likely cause to be faulty root action, usually due to waterlogged soil rotting the roots; this has to be avoided by planting the trees in well-drained ground in the first place. Other causes are bacterial canker (see above) or fireblight (see below).

False silver leaf is a nutritional disorder that can easily be confused with silver leaf (see below), but it simply means that the tree is short of fertilizer; the foliage shows the silvery sheen but most leaves on the tree are affected at once and there is no dieback nor is there the typical stain in the wood. An immediate foliar feed should correct the deficiency quite quickly.

Fireblight is caused by a bacteria that enters through the flowers, more likely in pears than other tree fruits. Although eradication measures taken nationally over the last thirty years or so have now reduced the risk, the disease is really only just contained. It can attack cotoneasters, hawthorns, pyracanthas, and other garden plants and spread from them to fruit trees. The immediate effect is like a scorching of the leaves from fire, causing them to wither but remain hanging on while the wood dies. If you suspect fireblight you must obtain expert advice at once, in fairness to your neighbours, and be prepared to burn the tree.

Frosts in winter seldom damage the hardy fruit trees described in this book; but spring frosts can so damage fruit blossom that it never sets to form fruitlets. A ground frost occurs when the earth's surface and the air just above it cools to 32°F (0°C). An air frost occurs when the air temperature at 4 ft (1.2 m) above ground level falls below freezing point. When nights are calm and cloudless the ground can cool rapidly by radiation heat loss but low cloud acts as a natural blanket and checks this, so frost is then unlikely. The water in the fruit blossoms, or the tender shoots of softer plants, may then freeze and thaw rapidly in the morning sun, bursting their cell walls in the process. As cold air flows downhill it can collect in front of hedges or walls and form a frost pocket, obviously not a place in which to plant fruit trees. Sloping ground from which cold air will drain away is much safer. There is no cure for frost so the best prevention is to drop polythene or a fine-mesh net over a bush or wall-trained tree at blossom time when frost seems likely, preferably so supported that it does not touch the blossoms. To check if fruit blossom has been frost damaged, pick off the middle one in a cluster and split it with your thumb-nail; if frosted it will be brown.

Gumming, which can exude from branches of cherry, plum, and other stone fruits, may be a response to damage of various kinds and is best left alone. If, however, it occurs fairly extensively on a tree bacterial canker may be the problem (see pages 51–2). Gumming may also indicate a faulty soil condition.

Honey fungus (*Armillaria mellea*) is a root parasite that spreads underground from decaying tree stumps by sending out black rhizomorphs or 'bootlaces'. These infest living roots and eventually kill them. The fungus creeps up under the bark to look like fine-mesh black netting and wood so infected by the living spores of honey fungus is curiously luminous at night. The rot is also spread by spores from edible toadstools with long yellow stems and honey-coloured caps with brown scales. If these are seen, start at once by removing completely the dead stump and roots on which they are living for immediate burning. Then fork outwards to pick up every bit of the fungus before it can spread further; although eradication is difficult it can be helped by sterilizing the

The toadstools from which the spores of the honey fungus are spread

soil with a recommended specific. Prevention consists of always removing stumps completely and never cutting trees off at ground level, leaving the roots to rot. Old apple trees are among the major culprits if their roots are left in the ground when being grubbed out.

June drop is a phenomenon well known to growers of apples and pears, who find a full crop of fruitlets suddenly dropping some of them, somewhat alarmingly. It is possibly nature's way of reducing a prospective overload to proportions with which the tree can cope or it may be the result of incomplete pollination, often accelerated by climatic conditions. Many crops will need thinning anyway, following a generous set of blossom, but it is best first to see the finish of the June crop, which can happen in July in a late season, before doing this. When a cluster of three apple flowers successfully sets all three the middle one is called the 'king' apple and has a short, stubby stalk. If all three survive the June drop the king should be dethroned anyway as it will not store well and may push off one or both of the others as it swells.

Nutrient shortages show recognizable signs on the foliage that indicate the action to take for correction.

Nitrogen deficiency is shown by the pale greenish colour of the leaves, which turn yellowish in extreme cases, first on the older foliage (which is often smaller than usual). Growth may be poor or even stunted and the fruits will be small, although highly coloured. This shortage is corrected by applying, early in the growing season, a nitrogen-containing fertilizer such as sulphate of ammonia or rotted farmyard manure.

The characteristic effect of manganese deficiency on apple leaves

Phosphorus deficiency is shown when the foliage turns a dull blue-green or purplish colour, older leaves being affected first and probably being smaller than they should be. Apply superphosphate fertilizer.

Potassium deficiency is indicated if the edges of the leaves curl up and go brown, as if scorched, with brown patches on the undersides, older leaves being affected first. Bonfire ash is full of potassium and this can be pricked-in over the roots and watered down or sulphate-of-potash fertilizer can be applied. An excess of potash, however, can upset the balance so that fruit is produced at the expense of young growth.

Magnesium deficiency shows as a yellowing between the veins of the leaves, giving a marbling effect, and is more likely with apples than other fruits.

Manganese deficiency is sometimes a problem on wet, organic soil and is also shown by a yellowing between the veins of older leaves but usually with additional dead patches; younger leaves may be rolled upwards.

If you suspect one of these two deficiencies it is best to show typical leaves to an expert before buying any fertilizers.

Papery bark is caused by waterlogged soil at the roots. The bark becomes papery thin and peels off, followed by dieback. Treatment is to prune away affected branches, scraping the area if on the main stem and painting on fungicidal paint. Drainage is likely to be in need of improvement.

Peach leaf curl attacks outdoor peaches, nectarines, almonds, and sometimes apricots. It seldom affects trees grown under glass or polythene. As the leaves appear in spring they develop blisters, at first

Peach leaf curl

green or yellow, later turning red, with a curling of the foliage. A white bloom later indicates the production of fungus and the removal of infected leaves before this stage is reached will check the disease. The tree produces more foliage, which is usually free of problems, but the process weakens it and over several years it can gradually be killed by these annual setbacks. From about the turn of the year until mid-May spores are spread by rain splash and if they settle on developing buds the resulting foliage will be infected, the disease being more likely after a cold wet spring. It therefore follows that if a tree can be protected from the rain by some sort of polythene cover the risk of leaf curl disease can be eliminated.

Pear leaf blister mite is a tiny pest causing pale pink or green blotches on leaves in May. These later turn brown or black. Control is difficult and may not be necessary unless shoots become distorted and affect the tree's vigour. The most helpful action is to collect and burn affected leaves.

Pear midge may first be evident when young fruitlets drop in early summer, probably distorted and containing very small, yellow grubs. Chemical treatment is hardly effective and the best solution is to rake up and burn the fallen fruitlets to prevent another attack next year; an insecticide dust worked into the soil under the tree should help.

Pear suckers are aphids that feed on developing buds, causing them to turn brown, and leave honeydew and sooty mould on the leaves .

Powdery mildew can affect most fruit trees but is more serious on apples and usually indicates that the roots are too dry. It is noticeable in spring, as emerging shoots and leaves appear covered in dusty grey powder due to a layer of fungus spores; these are released from May to September,

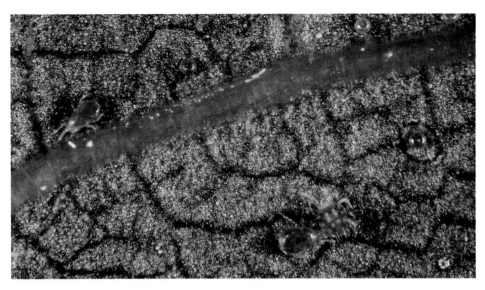

Typhlodronius pyri, a natural predator, attacking red spider mite

especially in June, when they infect next year's buds. The prompt removal of mildewed leaves and shoots into a polythene bag as soon as noticed in spring is the most effective control. This can be done again later in summer if secondary infection is noticed, but watering and mulching by then may have avoided it. After an outbreak it is best to spray in the following spring and summer with a systemic fungicide.

Red spider mites are seldom a problem on unsprayed trees because they are kept at bay by natural predators, but they can become a nuisance on plum and apple trees in hot dry seasons. They are not really spiders and are brown rather than red, only to be seen with a magnifying glass on the undersides of the leaves, together with their minute eggs, from late June onwards. They suck sap from the leaves, which become discoloured and dry up before falling prematurely; early removal of these leaves may provide sufficient control. Spraying against mildew should also deal with red spider mites. As leaves severely infested by red spider mites can turn silvery in colour, this can then be mistaken for silver leaf disease, but white skins cast by spider mites may be spotted on the undersides.

Replant disease can occur when a young tree is planted in the soil formerly occupied by an older tree of the same species whose roots have been growing there for some years. The latter, before removal, will probably have got its feeding roots into fresh soil well away from the stem, leaving the ground in the middle impoverished or even infected. It is important to plant young trees in fresh ground, or at least to remove impoverished soil and replace it with top soil from another part of the garden which has not grown similar trees, perhaps with peat incorporated. It has been proved that most tree fruits and particularly apples can be affected by replant disease unless planted in fresh or sterilized soil.

Rust on plum leaves

Various pathological suggestions for replant disease have been put forward, such as viruses, either soil-borne or transmitted by eelworms, but it is most likely to be caused by a microscopic, soil-inhabiting fungus called pythium. This attacks the root of a new plant faster than the plant can make new rootlets to grow away from it. Resting the soil is not the answer, as the fungus can remain in the soil for years.

Root suckers can appear below the graft from the rootstock and must be removed cleanly as soon as noticed. They will attract sap from the roots before branches higher up and quickly grow to the detriment of the tree, quite uselessly. It is best to pull away the soil from the stem to disclose the source of the sucker and to tear it away cleanly. If you have to cut it off, use a sharp knife and leave none of it behind or it will simply grow again with renewed vigour. Figs are not normally grafted plants and so their 'suckers' are from their own roots.

Rust mainly affects plums, but it also sometimes attacks peaches. It can be identified by the bright yellow spots on the upper sides of the leaves, with brown dusty patches beneath containing the fungus spores. Leaves turn yellow and fall prematurely, weakening a tree already not at its best, and must be gathered for burning. The tree needs attention – which means watering, mulching, and feeding to get it into healthy growth again.

Sawfly are so called because their larvae have piercing and cutting 'teeth' that enable them to tunnel into the fruit from the side, unlike the codling which enters through the eye. The female apple sawfly lays her eggs in the blossom and the white grubs crawl over the fruitlets, nibbling just below the skin and leaving ribbon-like scars before they enter, usually from the side. Badly damaged fruitlets drop off and the fully-fed larvae also drop to

Apples damaged by sawfly

the ground in July to pupate in the soil. It helps to limit later attacks if infested fruits are picked off and destroyed in June. You can apply a routine spray to kill sawfly and codling at the same time – that is, about a week after full blossoming and again, soon after, as the petals drop.

The plum sawfly acts in similar fashion, laying eggs on the flowers in April which hatch into caterpillars a fortnight later and these tunnel into the fruitlets. You can spray to kill the caterpillars before they tunnel into the plums and hoeing the soil under infested trees can reduce the population surviving to next year.

Scab is a fungus disease of apple and pear trees, sometimes of peaches, which can affect both the leaves, which form dark, rounded, dusty blotches, and the fruits, which develop scabby cracks and blisters, usually only skin-deep so that they can still be eaten if peeled. Some varieties, notably 'Cox's Orange Pippin', are more prone to scab than others, especially if the soil is heavy and badly drained or manurial treatment is incorrect. A systemic fungicide spray, applied fortnightly from bud-burst to blossom fall, is an effective preventative measure. Young shoots can also develop pimples like blisters which turn to cracks and scabs; these and all affected leaves should be collected up and burnt during the autumn so that over-wintering stages of the fungus are destroyed. A suitable spray programme should be followed the next spring and summer, following expert advice.

Shot hole, as the name implies, looks like round gunshot holes in the leaves, mainly on peaches and cherries. Initial light brown patches die off, leaving the perforations; the cause may be physiological but the problem is not serious and the cure is probably to pay attention to drainage and nutrition.

Shot hole on a cherry leaf

Silver leaf can affect other tree fruits but is prevalent on plums, especially 'Victoria'. Following a wound of some sort a parasite can cause a fungus to produce a toxic substance in the sap; the leaves develop a silvery sheen, caused by air in the tissues, and shoots die off progressively as the disease works back along the branch. As an infected branch thickens it will show a purplish stain in the centre when cut across and pruning away diseased wood is the first step to take, cutting back until an unstained cross section is reached. Sometimes the bark of the tree, especially an older one, may bear flat, purplish fungal growths, usually on dead wood, and this must be removed for burning.

The disease is incurable but can be halted by the above surgery and by treating exposed surfaces with fungicidal paint. If silver leaf has gone unnoticed until it has reached the main trunk of the tree then it must be dug out completely, root and all. There is, however, an optimistic note to be struck in that trees only lightly infected can sometimes throw off silver leaf disease, although dead branches will not, of course, revive and must be cut off and burnt.

As has been mentioned plums, cherries and other stone fruits should not be pruned in winter when disease is more likely to enter through cuts, which is how silver leaf gets a hold, it is generally believed. Any fractured branch should be trimmed off neatly at once and the exposed surface treated with fungicidal paint. Branches which become heavily laden with fruit must be supported to prevent breakages that can let in disease.

Slugworm feeding on the soft tissue of a leaf

Slugworms are the larvae of a species of sawfly and look like small slugs except that they have numerous legs like caterpillars and vary in colour from yellow to black. They feed on both surfaces of the leaves of cherries and pears, mostly, and skeletonize them. The best treatment is to pick them off into a jar of paraffin or petrol when seen or to apply insecticide.

Sooty mould can form on the leaves of pear and plum trees as a result of an attack by aphids or similar pests such as pear suckers.

Tortrix moth caterpillars can appear on fruit-tree foliage and fruitlets and are small, fast-moving yellow grubs, best picked off as soon as seen, before they spin themselves inside leaves for protection, making themselves difficult to touch with contact sprays. If using a systemic spray against codling this should also control tortrix. Cherry bark tortrix caterpillars, pinkish-brown with black heads, feed on the leaves like others; they also get into cracks under loose bark which can be scraped in March to disclose them.

Viruses, of which there are believed to be fifteen or more of some importance, are invisible and often latent, in which case they show no symptoms. Some viruses diminish the crop, some suppress growth, others put blemishes on the fruit or reduce its quality. They can be latent in some cultivars, yet produce severe symptoms in others. The longer a variety is

The caterpillar of the tortrix moth on an apple leaf

in cultivation the more likely it is to be attacked by one or more viruses that cause a gradual decline in vigour over a number of years as they build up. Once they are infected by viruses plants cannot be cured of them as they move in the sap and their vegetative progency will also be infected.

Some viruses are spread by aphids from old, infected trees nearby so a certain measure of control is achieved by preventing these from attacking fruit trees. British research stations have in recent years perfected ways of artificially freeing rootstocks and mother trees from these viruses so that reputable fruit tree nurserymen nowadays take their rootstocks or cutting material from virus-free stoolbeds or hedges and their grafting wood from 'clean' mother tree plantations. Nurseries and garden centres should now only sell virus-free trees and state this in their catalogues. These are therefore the trees to buy and they are likely to have a long and fruitful life, given sensible management in the garden.

Wind damage to branches, tragic if it happens when they are heavily laden in autumn, can be avoided by thinning the fruit in July. Otherwise, clothes-line props may be necessary or rope supports from higher branches.

Winter moth caterpillars attack in early spring to nibble the young leaves, buds, and blossom, particularly of apples. They have legs only at front and back ends, looping their bodies when moving, and hatch out from late April, frequently fastening leaves together. They feed until May or June and then drop to the ground on a silk thread to pupate until the next year. If leaves take on a ragged and holed appearance, look for these green or brown caterpillars with their arched back stance and pick them

A pear tree damaged by too-heavy cropping

off into a jar of paraffin or petrol. If you spot the damaged leaves but can find no sign of caterpillars, birds might have already eaten them or they may have dropped down to pupate. The best treatment is to apply grease bands around the stem of each tree every October; these trap the wingless female moths as they climb up from the ground to lay their eggs.

Trouble-shooting

'My tree never flowered.'
- No fruit buds, over-vigorous growth.
- Birds pecked out the fruit buds.
- Biennial bearer in its 'off' year.
- Tree too young; vigorous rootstock.
- Faulty pruning.
- Incorrect feeding.
- Planted with graft below ground.
- Poor plant or very poor soil.

'My tree flowered but has no fruit.'
- Blossom got frosted.
- Blossom was never pollinated.
- Leaves infected by powdery mildew.
- Roots are too dry; grass or over-hanging trees.
- Blossom wilt.

'My tree set fruit but many dropped off.'
- June drop.
- Disease; brown rot etc.
- Pest-ridden; sawfly etc.
- Incorrect feeding or drought.

APPLES

Apple trees probably originated in the wild as long ago as 6,500 BC, according to carbon-dated evidence from Anatolia. The Stone Age lake dwellers of central Europe certainly ate apples and, as remains found in their habitations show, also preserved them by drying. Cultivation of the apple started with the beginning of agriculture. Improved forms were selected from the forests of Asia Minor and spread around the Fertile Crescent. They were certainly being grown in the 13th century BC by the Egyptians in the Nile Valley.

Apples are frequently mentioned in Greek and Roman literature. In the *Odyssey*, written in the 9th century BC, Homer describes an orchard of apples, pears, and other fruits and the philosopher Theophrastus records a number of apple varieties grown in Greece round about 300 BC.

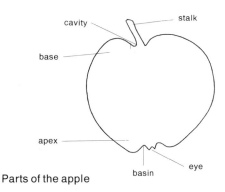

Parts of the apple

Crab apples probably came originally from Siberia, northern China, and Manchuria and have been cultivated in China and Japan since very earliest times. *Malus baccata*, the Siberian crab, has played an important part in the breeding of modern apples; it has been crossed with large-fruited cultivars in the search for hardiness and resistance to disease. The crab apples that became indigenous to most of Europe belong to the very variable species *M. pumila* or to *M. silvestris*. The well-known present-day crab apple 'John Downie' is a variety of *M. pumila*.

APPLES IN BRITAIN

The earliest-known English apple, recorded in a Norfolk deed of 1204, is the pear-shaped 'Pearmain', used for dessert and cider. Nearly as old is 'Costard', mentioned in deeds of 1296 and 1325 and still popular in Shakespeare's time. Costermongers take their name from this apple; they were originally sellers of Costards, at 4d per hundred in the late 15th century.

The oldest variety of apple in the collection of the National Fruit Trials is 'Decio', which, legend would have us believe, was introduced from central Italy in the middle of the 5th century by a Roman general named Ezio. 'Isaac Newton's Tree', or rather its descendant, is another old cultivar maintained in the same collection. The tree, whose falling apple led Newton to the idea of universal gravitation, was believed, rather uncertainly, to be a variety called 'Flower of Kent'. Before the original tree died grafts were taken and the progeny renamed in honour of Sir Isaac. Another old tree that survives today is 'Keswick Codling', an early-season cooker dating from 1793.

Apple identification

Pomologists have often attempted to produce systems of classification to make identification of apples easier. A fairly simple method, proposed by Edward Bunyard (1878–1939), is the basis of the system used today by the National Fruit Trials and applied in the descriptions that follow. Under this system apples are classified, according to the appearance of the mature fruit, into eight groups:

GROUP I Smooth-skinned, green, sour culinary apples ('Lord Derby'-type).

GROUP II Smooth-skinned, green, sweet dessert apples ('Granny Smith'-type).

GROUP III Smooth-skinned, striped, sour culinary apples ('Lane's Prince Albert'-type).

GROUP IV Smooth-skinned, flushed or striped, sweet dessert apples ('James Grieve'-type).

GROUP V Yellow-skinned dessert and culinary apples ('Golden Noble'-type).

GROUP VI Mainly red, mainly dessert apples ('Worcester Pearmain'-type).

GROUP VII Reinettes, dessert apples, skin coloured with some russet ('Cox's Orange Pippin'-type).

GROUP VIII Dessert apples with skin mainly russet ('Egremont'-type).

To identify an unknown apple, take a typical ripe fruit from the tree, determine which of the eight group descriptions best fits it, decide, by referring to the diagram (opposite above), what shape it is, and consider in which month it is in prime season. You may, for example, have a smooth-skinned cooking

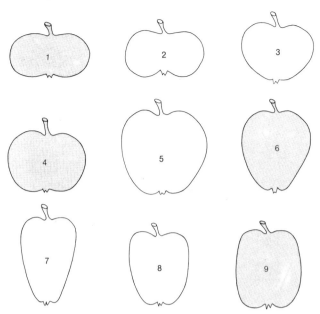

Apple shapes – 1 flat; 2 flat-round; 3 short-round-conical; 4 round; 5 round-conical; 6 conical; 7 long-conical; 8 oblong-conical; 9 oblong

apple. It fits the description of Group I. It is 'round'. Its season is August. The table (page 146) will tell you that it is 'Grenadier'.

Awards

For many years, the Royal Horticultural Society has accepted fruits for awards. The raiser or the introducer (usually a nurseryman) of a new fruit tree may enter it for the Award of Merit (A.M.) or for the higher award of First Class Certificate (F.C.C.). I include these awards and their dates in my descriptions. There are, of course, worthy cultivars that have never been submitted for an award, particularly some that were in existence before the scheme started.

Old British apples

The best-known of the classic apples are described here in the approximate order of their introduction, up to the end of the 19th century. These apples were mostly chance seedlings and the seed, or female, parent has usually been recorded but it was only towards the end of this period that the pollen, or male, parent, even if known, was thought to be important.

Court Pendu Plat (Group VII) may claim to be the oldest apple still in cultivation; it has been known for at least four hundred years, perhaps even from Roman times. It has probably survived so long because it flowers very late, missing frosts, keeps well into spring, and resists disease. The apples are small, in colour dull red overlying yellow, but richly flavoured. It does well on heavy soils but needs another late-flowering apple as a pollinator.

Devonshire Quarrenden (Group VI), an old West Country favourite known by the fruit scholar and writer John Worlidge in 1678 and possibly of French origin, has crimson apples in September. I was sad to lose my tree when widening a drive some years ago, even though it was biennial and rather cankerous, because it tolerated any amount of unfavourable weather.

Ribston Pippin (Group VII) was raised from seed brought from Rouen in Normandy to Ribston Hall, Knaresborough, Yorkshire, the home of Sir Henry Goodricke, and sown by the gardener there, Robert Clemesha. This was probably in 1707, the year of Sir Henry's marriage. The original tree blew over between 1810 and 1815, and was damaged by cattle, but it lived on and fruited for another twenty years, supported by props. A short portion of the old trunk remained and a replacement shoot sprouted from below soil level. Carefully preserved, and protected by an iron fence, this grew on until a gale toppled it in November 1928. The stump finally gave up the struggle in 1932. 'Ribston Pippin' is one of the richest-flavoured apples when fully ripe in November; it keeps well into January, but loses flavour after that. A triploid variety, it makes a big tree and needs to spread its roots far to pick up moisture, so these days it should be grown on a dwarfing rootstock. Its fruits are yellow with a browny-red flush and some russetting, sweet, and aromatic. It received its Award of Merit in 1962, a time lag that is not uncommon with these old varieties.

Ashmead's Kernel (Group VIII), according to most sources, was raised in Gloucester in about 1720 by a local physician, Dr Ashmead. I can find no evidence of Dr Ashmead's existence, although a property later named Ashmead House still stands on the north side of Eastgate Street. William Ashmead (1721–82), who was an attorney living or working at this address, acquired the property from a John Ashmead (who was not a doctor) in 1758. Soon after, the propagation of this apple must have been entrusted to Mr Wheeler, of Kingsholm, Gloucester, because I have a description of a tree standing in Wheeler's nursery in 1796 that had been grafted from the original over thirty years before. This was perhaps the mother tree from which Wheeler distributed trees around the county and further afield, from 1780, through the Brompton Park Nursery in London. 'Ashmead's Kernel' has very beautiful

'Ashmead's Kernel'

blossom and superbly flavoured apples, much liked by tasting panels, from December on. The greeny-yellow skin has a red-brown flush and is russetted and scab-resistant. The tree is a somewhat shy bearer, but it has, nonetheless, had a revival of popularity in recent years, even gaining an Award of Merit in 1969 and its First Class Certificate in 1981. It is well worth trying as a cordon on a dwarf stock.

Blenheim Orange (Group VII) was raised about 1740 by Mr Kempster, a tailor of Woodstock, Oxfordshire, in his garden near the park of Blenheim Palace. It set a new standard of quality and is a name much respected in pomology. It was not shown to the Royal Horticultural Society until 1822, but then became better known and is now grown widely, even outside Britain, in America and Australia. Edward Bunyard wrote of 'Blenheim Orange' in *The Anatomy of Dessert* that 'impatient youth or those of riper years should

choose a variety which comes sooner to profit' and certainly on the rootstocks available in 1929 it was slow to come into bearing. Grown on the modern dwarfer rootstocks, however, as recommended for other triploid varieties, it begins to fruit early in its life and to overcome its biennial tendency. Favoured both for dessert and cooking, Blenheims are large, orange-yellow apples with a distinctive nutty flavour, ready from November onwards. Smaller Blenheims once went to the dining room to be enjoyed with the port and a slice of cheese, while the larger ones went to the kitchen to be made into apple charlotte.

Orleans Reinette (Group VII) competes with 'Blenheim Orange' and 'Ribston Pippin' and has similarities to both, being somewhat biennial. Bunyard thought it came from the Low Countries about 1776, suggesting that 'if Rembrandt had painted a fruit piece he would have chosen this apple', a reference to its brown-red flush on glowing gold skin. Perhaps it has more russet than 'Blenheim' and a rather nuttier

'Blenheim Orange'

Blossom of 'Bramley's Seedling'

flavour than 'Ribston'. Its season is also later, competing with 'Cox's Orange Pippin' from December on into March in careful storage, as it can shrivel if too warm. Nearing harvest it needs watching in order to pick on the right day, before it drops. It won an Award of Merit in 1914 under its old name of 'Winter Ribston' and another in 1921 as 'Orleans Reinette'.

D'Arcy Spice (Group VIII) was discovered growing in the garden of The Hall, Tolleshunt D'Arcy, near Colchester, Essex, in about 1785 and was for long much esteemed in East Anglia. It became more widely known, but under the name 'Baddow Pippin', later found to be a synonym, when re-introduced in 1848 by John Harris, a nurseryman of Great Baddow, Essex. It must be said, however, that outside that area it seldom finds a soil to its liking or the hot, dry summer it prefers and away from its homeland it often slowly makes a weakish tree. The apple has a short stem deeply inserted into a russet cavity and greeny-yellow skin with heavy russetting. The flesh is firm, crisp, aromatic, and of fine quality; the apples need careful storing if they are to be kept to their full potential in March or even later.

Bramley's Seedling (Group III) was grown from a pip sown in her parents' garden in Church Street, Southwell, Nottingham, by Mary Ann Brailsford, between 1809, when her father, Charles Brailsford, bought the property, and 1813, when she left home to marry. The property was bought in January 1846 by a local butcher and publican, Matthew Bramley, and it was during his ownership that Henry Merryweather, son of the head gardener at nearby Norwood Hall, took

grafts from the tree and started to sell young trees from his newly established nursery in Southwell. He also exhibited the apples to the Royal Horticultural Society in December 1876, when they won an Award of Merit. H. Bradley of nearby Halam, raiser of the 'Bradley's King' damson, also exhibited 'Bramley's Seedling' apples and in 1893 they won a First Class Certificate. The original tree fell in about 1915; in 1922 it was surviving with the lower part of its stem horizontal on the ground and it was still living in 1945.

'Bramley's Seedling' is the most widely grown cooker in Britain. It is a triploid with a tendency to biennial bearing; for garden planting it should be grown on a dwarfing rootstock, as otherwise it makes a big tree. The large green and red apples, particularly good for baking and a favourite for dumplings, are rich in vitamin C and keep well in store from November to February. Bramleys cook to a creamy purée, the sharp taste and fruity flavour combining well with pastry; earlier windfalls cook to a froth and taste even sharper because of their greater acidity. 'Crimson Bramley' is a well-known, more highly coloured clone.

Cox's Orange Pippin (Group VII), surely the best-known apple in Britain, was raised from a pip sown in about 1825 by Richard Cox, a retired brewer, in the grounds of Lawn Cottage, Colnbrook, Middlesex. The first trees propagated from the original seedling, which eventually blew down in 1911, were sold locally by the nursery of E. Small and Son of Colnbrook in about 1840, but the variety was taken up by Charles Turner of the Royal Nurseries, Slough, in about 1850. Charles Turner believed that the seedling had been one grown from pips of 'Ribston Pippin'

'Cox's Orange Pippin'

soil where the drainage is too free and also heavier, poorly drained soil – although they succeed in the clay belts of Sussex and East Anglia when well drained. A high lime content upsets them. If they are overfed with nitrogen, the fruits lack colour and will not store long and the trees become susceptible to scab and canker; if they are short of nitrogen, the apples lack size and flavour and lose their aroma, the skins being too highly coloured and the flesh white rather than yellow. In other words, 'Cox's Orange Pippin' needs the right soil and good management if apples of the standard of those grown on English orchards are to be picked.

Golden Noble (Group V) is a large cooking apple with few equals in its season. It is believed to have been discovered growing locally by Patrick Flanagan, gardener to Sir Thomas Hare of Stowe Hall, Downham, Norfolk, and to have been introduced in 1820. The fruits are golden-yellow with green flecks and grey russet, ready for October to December use; in a pie they cook perfectly by the time the pastry is ready. Bunyard's experience with this tree was that it does not thrive on all soils and it has a reputation for light cropping, which may be why it is not widely grown.

King of the Pippins (Group VII) has gone out of favour today and was probably better known as an orchard standard. The true fruit, which has a bitter-sweet flavour, is yellowy-orange streaked with red; it is ready in November, but biennial. Stocks may have got muddled in the past. It was named by Joseph Kirke of the Brompton nursery early in the 19th century; he is thought to have got it from Belgium, where Bunyard thought it was known as 'Krönen Reinette' before 1800. It may also be identical to the French 'Reine des Reinettes' and to 'Golden Winter Pearmain'.

Rosemary Russet (Group VII) is an old English apple that was first recorded in 1831. It is another valuable dessert variety of good quality that crops generously when well grown, although the apples can be a little small unless thinned. It is hardly ready to eat before late November and keeps until March in careful storage, the fruits being yellowy-brown with some russetting and a deep red flush; they have long stalks. The juicy, creamy-white flesh is rather acid, with an excellent flavour that is not typically russet. Bunyard, always the epicure, thought of it as one of the best apples for late winter desserts.

Lane's Prince Albert (Group III) was raised in about 1840 by Thomas Squire of Berkhamsted from 'Russet Nonpareil' pollinated by 'Dumelow's Seedling'. It was introduced in 1850 and gained its First Class Certificate

apple. His son, Arthur, who succeeded his father at the Royal Nurseries, was reported as telling a friend that he thought the seed parent, 'Ribston Pippin', had been pollinated by a 'Blenheim Orange'.

Apples of 'Cox's Orange Pippin' won first prize at the Royal Horticultural Society's Grand Fruit Exhibition in October 1857, beating 'Ribston Pippin'. At the National Apple Congress organized by the society in 1883, no fewer than 183 out of 231 exhibitors showed it, a measure of the popularity the apple had obtained by then. Nonetheless, 'Cox's Orange Pippins' had to wait until 1962 before being awarded a First Class Certificate.

Bunyard recommended that 'Cox's Orange Pippin' be kept for dessert from November to January but that 'for eating between meals, or in the morning, an apple less of a sweetmeat be chosen'.

'Cox's Orange Pippin' and its more highly coloured clone, 'Queen Cox', are now popular in British commercial orchards, which produced just under 110,000 tons (100,000 tonnes) of these two apples in 1987. It must be said, however, that neither is an easy apple for amateurs to grow; they are best left to the commercial orchard growers. They dislike both light in 1872. A bush tree that I planted over forty years ago still provided me in 1987 with over three hundred cooking apples; I find they store easily into March, by which time they have become acceptable for dessert. The fruit is green, with bright red stripes on the sunny side, the flesh soft and acid, gradually sweetening with age. The tree is very compact in growth and best grafted on to the semi-dwarfing rootstock MM.106; it can suffer from a form of canker that is difficult to control but seems not to be fatal.

Sturmer Pippin (Group II) was raised by Ezekiel Dillistone, a nurseryman of Sturmer, near Haverhill, Suffolk, and first recorded in 1841. It is believed to be a seedling of 'Ribston Pippin' pollinated by 'Nonpareil'. Bunyard thought it an indispensable dessert apple for very late eating in April or May, adding that 'it is as digestable as india rubber if gathered too early'. It needs a hot summer and to be left on the tree as late as possible, even into November or December. The apples are yellowish-green with a brown flush and some grey russet. The flesh is yellow, firm, crisp, and juicy, and slow to mature. The tree is of compact habit only. Ezekiel Dillistone's grandson, Thomas, emigrated to Australia taking grafting wood with him; in 1934 about 800,000 bushels (2,200 hl) of Sturmers were exported from Australia to Britain.

Beauty of Bath (Group IV), said to be a seedling of 'Juneating', was raised at Bailbrook, near Bath, and introduced in about 1864. It was awarded its First Class Certificate in 1887. It is an early August apple which tends to start dropping its crop before it ripens fully and to need thinning for apples of decent size. The flesh is white, tinged with red, pleasant when ripe but quickly past its best. The skin is yellow, heavily striped with red streaks and numerous red dots.

Lord Derby (Group I) was raised by a nurseryman in Stockport, Cheshire, and named after that Lord Derby who was three times British prime minister between 1852 and 1868. It was first recorded in 1862. It is a cooking apple that grows robustly, thriving on heavy soil and resisting scab. It also fruits regularly, in which it is probably helped by the fact that it flowers late and so misses frosts. The large apples are green, turning yellow when mature in November and into December, and the flesh is firm and yellow, cooking golden-red.

Peasgood's Nonsuch (Group IV) is a cooking apple that was raised by Mrs Peasgood of Stamford, Lincolnshire, in about 1858, from a pip of 'Catshead Codling'. It is a very fertile variety that grows large apples for the season September to December and is often used for baking and also for exhibiting. It received a First Class Certificate in 1872. The colour is attractive, golden-yellow, flushed bright crimson, and the flesh is yellow and tender, cooking to a froth.

Annie Elizabeth (Group III) is a cooker raised by Samuel Greatorex at Knighton, Leicester, and named after his daughter, who died in 1866, aged only thirteen months. His apple received a First Class Certificate in 1868; it was shown by Harrison and Sons of Leicester, who apparently delayed introduction until 1898. They believed it to have been raised from 'Blenheim Orange' but Robert Hogg, in his *Herefordshire Pomona*, thought it may have been a seedling of 'Bess Pool'. It flowers late, the fruits being pale yellow in colour, flushed and striped brilliant red, keeping well into December and much later if required. The flesh is crisp, white, and acid, breaking up when cooked. It makes a hardy, upright tree of compact habit that crops regularly and is suitable for growing in the north of England.

Grenadier (Group I) was first recorded in 1862 and introduced about 1875, receiving a First Class

'Grenadier'

Certificate in 1883. It is a popular early cooker, ready August and September. The smooth, pale green apples fade to yellow when ripe and are produced freely and regularly, the white flesh being crisp, juicy, and acid, cooking to a froth. The tree is of medium vigour, hardy, and resistant to scab. It is widely planted commercially, often as a pollinator for 'Bramley's Seedling' with a third cultivar to pollinate it.

Granny Smith (Group II) was raised from a chance seedling noticed by Mrs Thomas Smith of Ryde, New South Wales, Australia, in about 1860 and it is now widely grown there and in South Africa and New Zealand, where the climate suits it. Although extensively tested in England at the National Fruit Trials between 1935 and 1948, it cannot be grown commercially with any great success in northern Europe or in Britain and for garden planting the space is better given to a choicer cultivar. The dark green, greasy-skinned, and somewhat flavourless (albeit hard and juicy) apples are seen in the shops in late winter.

Egremont Russet (Group VIII) is not well documented but was recorded in John Scott's *Orchardist* in 1868,

the earliest date I can find. George Wyndham, Earl of Egremont (born in 1751), may have raised it on his Sussex estate at Petworth early in the 19th century. He is known to have been interested in producing new russet apples in about 1790, together with his gardener, John Slade (who died in 1827). His papers, though, were apparently all destroyed on his death. It is now widely grown in orchards – it is a good pollinator for 'Cox's Orange Pippin' – but it is also popular in gardens because it makes a neat, upright bush or a good cordon and forms spurs well. It is scab resistant, but can suffer from bitter pit. It won its Award of Merit in 1980. The apples are golden-brown, with a covering of fine light-brown russet, and are ready to eat from October into December. The flesh is firm, greenish-yellow, and of nutty flavour, very good as dessert with a chunk of Cheddar cheese.

Worcester Pearmain (Group VI), believed to be a seedling of 'Devonshire Quarrenden', was raised by Mr Hale of Swan Pool, near Worcester, and introduced in 1874. It gained its First Class Certificate in the following year. The apples, best eaten off the tree when fully ripe, are bright crimson on a yellow ground

'Egremont Russet'

'Worcester Pearmain'

and the flesh is crisp and sweet and has a slight strawberry flavour. 'Worcester Pearmain' is a tip bearer which produces few spurs but it crops regularly and was formerly much planted in orchards – it is a good pollinator for 'Cox's Orange Pippin', as is 'Discovery', which is now largely replacing it.

'Merton Worcester' was introduced in 1947 as an alternative to 'Worcester Pearmain' for garden planting. It was raised at the John Innes Institution from Cox's 'Orange Pippin' × 'Worcester Pearmain', but it is not widely grown, being susceptible to bitter pit.

Newton Wonder (Group III) was found as a seedling, probably from 'Dumelow's Seedling' pollinated by 'Blenheim Orange', growing in the thatched roof of the Hardinge Arms at King's Newton, near Melbourne, Derbyshire. It was introduced by Pearson and Co. in about 1887, receiving a First Class Certificate in that year. It is a dual-purpose apple – at first a cooker, ready in November, but by March sweetened enough to become welcome for dessert. The colour is yellow with flush or broad stripes of scarlet and the flesh is greeny-white, firm, crisp, juicy, and subacid. It makes a big tree unless on a dwarfing rootstock and one I once owned I found also to be a biennial bearer; as it flowers late a suitable pollinator is essential.

Charles Ross (Group IV) – named after its raiser, a Scotsman who was head gardener at Welford Park Gardens, Newbury, Berkshire – is from 'Peasgood's Nonsuch' pollinated by 'Cox's Orange Pippin'. Introduced in 1890, it was at first named 'Thomas Andrew Knight', after the President of the Royal Horticultural Society, who had helped Charles Ross, but was given its present name at the request of Ross's employer, Captain Carstairs. It received its First Class Certificate in 1899. The fruit is a large and attractive apple, ready in late September and keeping into November, but not much later, flushed or striped orange-red on a greenish-yellow ground. The flesh is creamy-white, sweet, and fairly juicy, making either a good baked apple or a pleasant dessert. Not planted commercially, it makes a good garden tree of fairly upright growth that does well on thin soils over chalk and succeeds in the north of England.

James Grieve (Group IV) was raised by and named after another Scotsman, and introduced in about 1890

'Newton Wonder'

'James Grieve'

The blossom of 'James Grieve'

by the nursery of Dickson of Edinburgh, his employers. The Royal Horticultural Society's *Journal* for 1897, the year in which it gained its Award of Merit, stated that it was from 'Cox's Orange Pippin', open-pollinated, but Bunyard reported that it was raised from 'Pott's Seedling'. It received a First Class Certificate in 1906. The flowers are rich carmine and white, very fertile, and good for pollinating other cultivars. The yellow-skinned apples have a slight red flush and crimson stripes, variable but attractive on the tree. 'James Grieve' used to be grown commercially, partly as a very efficient pollinator for 'Cox's Orange Pippin', but it does not travel well and is now seldom seen in the shops. The flesh is yellow, tender, very juicy, and of excellent flavour, with a sharp, somewhat acid, taste, delightful eaten off the tree when ripe. An excellent garden tree, it can be put to culinary use if no cooker is grown for this season, normally from mid-September for a month or so.

Early Victoria (Group I) should correctly be called by its prior name, 'Emneth Early'. It was raised by William Lynn at Emneth, near Wisbech, Cambridgeshire, and introduced by Cross of Wisbech in 1899, winning an Award of Merit in the same year. Believed to be a seedling of 'Lord Grosvenor', pollinated by 'Keswick Codling', it is a very early cooker, ready at the end of July and lasting into September. The colour is yellowy-green, the flesh white, soft, and sub-acid, cooking to a froth, and it is the best of the true early codlings for crop, vigour, and appearance. It tends, though, to have small apples unless it is thinned and to crop biennially.

Early-20th-century apples

Not until toward the end of the 19th century did raisers of fruit trees become aware that the male, pollen-producing parent is just as important in providing the characteristics of the seedling offspring as is the female, seed-producing parent. Consequently, only from about the turn of the century have apples been introduced both of whose parents have been known and selected in a definite breeding programme. Of the cultivars so far described most have been either chance seedlings or open-pollinated, only the seed parent being known.

Thomas Andrew Knight was the first to raise seedlings whose full parentage was known. The twelve or more new apples he raised himself, although much grown at the time, have now been superseded, but his was the pioneer work that opened the way that other raisers followed when they saw what good new fruits could be produced by careful breeding.

For fruit trees (and in horticulture generally), the female or seed parent is always named first, followed by ' × ' and then the name of the male or pollen parent; this practice is the opposite to that used in human family trees. This information may often be of more than genealogical interest – a few apples fail to pollinate successfully with others that share a common parent.

Edward VII (Group I), first recorded in 1902, was named for the new king. Raised from 'Blenheim Orange' × 'Golden Noble', it received its Award of Merit in 1903 and was introduced by Rowe of Worcester in 1908. 'Edward VII' flowers very late and so can miss frosts, but it needs a suitable pollinator (see Flowering Table on page 150). The apples are green with a smooth and shiny skin, yellowing when ripe and keeping excellently in store until March or April. The flesh is cream, hard, and juicy and very acid, needing plenty of cooking, when it turns dark red and transparent.

Fortune (Laxton's) (Group VII) was raised by Laxton Brothers in 1904 from 'Cox's Orange Pippin' × 'Wealthy' and introduced by them in 1931, gaining an

Award of Merit in 1932 and a First Class Certificate in 1948. The apple is greeny-yellow, striped or flushed red, with a very pleasant sub-acid and aromatic flavour, perfect off the tree in October, but with a short season and, unfortunately, rather biennial in some areas. It makes a fairly compact tree and is suitable for the north of England, but may get scab in wet soils.

Reverend W. Wilks (Group V), named after a secretary of the Royal Horticultural Society, was raised and introduced by Veitch of Chelsea, from 'Peasgood's Nonsuch' × 'Ribston Pippin'. It gained an Award of Merit in 1904, followed in 1910 by a First Class Certificate. The fruit is unusual in becoming almost white when ripe and is fairly large with small streaks of clear red. It is primarily a cooker, ready late August to October, the flesh being white, sub-acid, and cooking to a yellow froth, but it can be used for dessert

'Lord Lambourne'

when ripe. Being a biennial bearer it should not be relied on as a pollinator, although as a compact grower it suits a small garden.

Ellison's Orange (Group VII) was raised jointly by the Reverend Charles C. Ellison, vicar of Bracebridge, near Lincoln, and Mr Wipf, gardener at Hartsholme Hall in Leicestershire, then the residence of Ellison's brother-in-law, who crossed 'Cox's Orange Pippin' with 'Calville Blanche'. It was first recorded as fruiting in 1904 and in 1908 Ellison wrote to leading fruit nurserymen announcing that between six hundred and a thousand grafts were to be sold to the highest bidder for the benefit of Mr Wipf. The successful buyers, Pennell and Sons of Lincoln, introduced it in 1911. It won an Award of Merit in that year, followed by a First Class Certificate in 1917. The apple is dull green with many red streaks, greasy when ripe, and long-stalked. It is ready early October and is very juicy off the tree but does not keep long. People tend to have definite opinions about the taste, which is often

described as like aniseed. It makes a good garden tree, although sometimes biennial. Its sport, 'Red Ellison', differs only in being more highly coloured.

Lord Lambourne (Group VII) was raised in 1907 by Laxton Brothers from 'James Grieve' × 'Worcester Pearmain', but not introduced until 1921. It won its Award of Merit in 1923. The apples are greeny-yellow, attractively flushed or striped red; they ripen in October, the flesh being sweet and juicy with pleasant flavour. 'Lord Lambourne' makes a good garden tree of moderate vigour and compact growth that has no bad faults and is very fertile, cropping regularly.

Epicure (Laxton's) (Group VII), although raised in 1909 from 'Wealthy' × 'Cox's Orange Pippin', was not introduced until 1929 and received its Award of Merit only in 1931. It is a regular cropper, usually needing thinning to get good-sized fruits. The apples are green with crimson streaks and long stalks, ready September, but not keeping long; the flesh is tender, juicy, and sweet and popular with children.

Arthur Turner (Group V) was raised by Charles Turner at Slough, Buckinghamshire, and introduced in 1912, when it received its Award of Merit. Its parentage seems to be unknown; it was at first named 'Turner's Prolific' but was renamed in 1913. In 1945 it received, somewhat unusually, an Award of Garden Merit for its blossom, which is particularly fine. It is a large apple for cooking, green with an orange-red flush, with a clear, polished skin, ready through September and into October. The flesh is creamy-white, somewhat dry and acid.

Golden Delicious (Group V) originated in the United States (see page 89). It is a pale yellow apple when ripe, flecked with a little russet, in season in Britain from November to February. The flesh is cream and crisp, juicy and a little acid, rather better when eaten at the right time from an English garden tree after a warm summer than when bought from a shop. 'Greensleeves' is an alternative.

Howgate Wonder (Group III) was raised in 1915 at Howgate Lane, Bembridge, Isle of Wight, by G. Wratton, from 'Blenheim Orange' × 'Newton Wonder'. It received an Award of Merit in 1929 and was introduced by Stuart Low and Co. in 1932. It is a large cooking apple, yellow-green, flushed and streaked red, often used for exhibition, which stores well for use from November to February. The flesh is creamy-white and juicy, breaking up when cooked. It is hardy, flowers late, and is moderately vigorous.

'Lord Lambourne' trained as a cordon

Sunset (Group VII), a seedling of 'Cox's Orange Pippin', open-pollinated, was raised about 1918 by G. C. Addy at Ightham, Kent. Its naming and introduction, by W. Rogers of Dartford, Kent, was delayed until 1933 and it received an Award of Merit in 1960 and a First Class Certificate in 1982. It is a high-quality dessert apple resembling 'Cox's Orange Pippin', than which it often does better on heavy soils. The fruit is greenish-yellow, becoming almost orange, and speckled with russet, usually a bit smaller than most dessert apples. I pick mine in mid-October for eating from November to December. The flesh is white, firm, and crisp, with the 'Cox's Orange Pippin' aromatic flavour. The habit of growth is compact and upright, which makes 'Sunset' a good garden tree.

Laxton's Superb (Group VII) – often shortened to either 'Superb' or 'Laxton' – was raised by Laxton Brothers in 1897 from 'Wyken Pippin' × 'Cox's Orange Pippin', but was not introduced until 1922, although it received an Award of Merit in 1919 and a First Class Certificate in 1921. It has greeny-yellow apples, about half covered with a reddish-purple flush and broken stripes, keeping well over a long season from November to February. The flesh is white, firm, very juicy, and sweet, with a refreshing flavour. The tree is biennial bearing, unfortunately, and of a rather spreading habit, with slender branches that spur freely.

Kidd's Orange Red (Group VII) was raised in 1924 from 'Cox's Orange Pippin' × 'Delicious' by J. H. Kidd in New Zealand, where it soon began to be grown commercially. It was shown to some growers in the

United Kingdom in about 1932, but they thought it unsuitable for market because of the amount of russet on the fruit. It was then forgotten in Britain until after World War II. English trials in 1954–64, however, showed it to be a good tree for gardens. It makes a useful alternative to 'Cox's Orange Pippin', being more resistant to scab and mildew. It received an Award of Merit in 1973. It makes spurs freely and is in season November to January; the apples are yellow, half or more covered in bright orange-scarlet flush and some stripes, with variable patches of russet. The flesh is creamy-white, firm, crisp, juicy, and sweet, with rich aromatic flavour.

Post-World War II apples

As research stations all over the world got back into their stride from 1946 onwards, promising new varieties began to be sent by their raisers and others for planting at the National Fruit Trials at Brogdale in Kent. These trials were carried out mainly for the benefit of commercial orchards, to help them plant the best and most suitable varieties for British markets. But perfectly good cultivars often prove to be unacceptable to commercial growers who, for economic reasons, have to grow big numbers of a few apples and for

'Crispin', fully ripened in the sun

whom 'Cox's Orange Pippin' and 'Bramley's Seedling' are still the favourites. These 'rejects' could often make desirable garden trees and provide a much greater range of flavours, but until the 1970s very little encouragement was given to retail nurseries to offer these new varieties to the public through their catalogues. This was especially the case after the closing of old-established firms like Rivers, Laxton, and Bunyard and the proliferation of garden centres, which normally sell plants only in pots. With the exception of apples grown on dwarf rootstocks, fruit trees are usually unhappy in the restricted root run of a pot, especially if stood too long before sale.

In recent years the patenting of new varieties has given fresh impetus to a few enterprising British nurseries to offer the newer apples and other fruits as they are released. Help from the research stations, East Malling in particular, and from the marketing agency, Plant Breeding International, Cambridge, in gaining publicity for these fruits, and the willingness of a few nurseries to exhibit at Royal Horticultural Society shows has encouraged a revival of interest in fruit growing. With the availability of dwarfing rootstocks more trees can be planted in any given area and the revived interest has included some of the older cultivars already described as well as the newer ones that follow.

Crispin (Group V) was raised at the Aomori Experimental Station in Japan from 'Golden Delicious' × 'Indo'. It first fruited in 1939 and under the name 'Mutsu' was received at the National Fruit Trials in Britain in 1953. Renamed 'Crispin', it was released in 1968 and received an Award of Merit in 1970. It is a green apple, resembling 'Golden Delicious'; when ripe it becomes yellow, with a slight purple flush. It is a triploid cultivar and can make a big tree, so is best grown on a dwarfing rootstock; because it makes spurs freely it is good as a cordon. It crops well in most years. The flesh is creamy-white, firm, juicy, a little sweet yet somewhat acid and refreshing. It is without great flavour, but I find this to be better if the apples are left on the tree for picking as late as possible; they store comfortably through the winter to February. 'Crispin' is not a pollinator, nor will 'Golden Delicious' pollinate it, but it has valuable apples for late winter dessert or cooking if required.

Spartan (Group VI) originated in Canada, where it was raised by R. C. Palmer at the Summerland Experiment Station in British Columbia from 'McIntosh' × 'Yellow Newtown'. It fruited for the first time in 1932 and trials in England started in 1960. The apples are a deep,

'Spartan'

bright purple colour almost completely covering a pale green ground and have an attractive bloom. The flesh is white, firm, crisp, and juicy, with a grapey flavour. A tree in my garden provides plenty of apples that taste far better than shop samples and have become family favourites for October and November – they will keep longer but we have usually eaten them by then. 'Spartan' makes spurs freely and crops well, though for good-sized apples it may need some thinning.

Gala (Group VI) was raised by J. H. Kidd in New Zealand, in about 1934, from 'Kidd's Orange Red' × 'Golden Delicious' and brought for trial in England in 1963. It has been taken up commercially in Britain and amateurs approve of it as an exhibition variety, but fruits have to be thinned to get apples of good size. They have a pale green ground partly flushed and flecked with bright scarlet, and some show a little grey russet. The cream flesh is firm, crisp, juicy, and fairly sweet, with an aromatic flavour. 'Gala' apples are delicious eaten off the tree, or they will keep in store from October to Christmas. A watch should be kept for scab in some areas.

A mutant, at first known as 'Royal Gala' but now renamed 'Tenroy', is an overall red-purple apple, sometimes stripey, with a similar flavour. It was bred

'Gala' grown in pots, above, and, below, trained as a single horizontal cordon

release in 1970. It is an extremely attractive, bright red apple with a shiny skin and a long stalk; the flesh is white, tinged with pink beneath the skin, a little soft, but juicy and sweet, with a pleasant flavour. It does not keep long, but is excellent for eating off the tree in September. It has a spreading, drooping habit, makes spurs freely, and crops heavily, often needing thinning.

Tydeman's Early Worcester (Group VI) was raised at East Malling Research Station by H. M. Tydeman from 'Worcester Pearmain' × 'McIntosh' in 1929, but not introduced until 1945. It is an earlier, and perhaps better, apple than its seed parent, but it stays in peak condition for only a very limited period. It has highly coloured fruits, richly flavoured and sweet, yet slightly acid.

Tydeman's Late Orange (Group VII) resulted from a breeding programme carried out at East Malling Research Station before World War II to find an alternative to 'Cox's Orange Pippin', although its introduction was delayed until 1949. 'Late Orange' (the name is often abbreviated) is from 'Laxton's Superb' × 'Cox's Orange Pippin'. It received an Award of Merit in 1965 and is now in a few catalogues, having proved to be a worthy garden tree. The apples are one-quarter to three-quarters flushed purplish-red on a yellow ground with some patches of russet. The flesh is almost yellow, very firm and crisp, fairly juicy with rich aromatic flavour. It keeps quite well in store for eating from December to March or later. The tree crops well, but may need thinning; its habit is fairly vigorous and spreading and it makes spurs readily.

Discovery (Group VI), from 'Worcester Pearmain', probably pollinated by 'Beauty of Bath', was raised by Mr Dummer of Langham, Essex, in about 1950. It was acquired by Jack Matthews, a notable fruit-tree grower of Thurston, Suffolk, who saw its possibilities and introduced it in 1963. I first grew 'Discovery' in 1967, by which time it was also in Holland, Switzerland, and France and already recognized as a most valuable new apple. It has masses of white blossom and fruits that are greenish-yellow, flushed half to three-quarters with bright red. The flesh is hard, crisp, sweet, juicy, and very chewy, in season from mid-August to mid-September, ahead of 'Worcester'. I consider 'Discovery' to be the earliest quality apple and worth waiting for, a delight eaten off the tree. It has the added value of being free with its fertile pollen – I guess that 'Discovery' now pollinates well over half the 'Cox's Orange Pippin' trees grown commercially. It is an easy, healthy variety to manage,

by the Delbard Nursery in France and is under trials in Britain, having already received a 'preliminary commendation' from the Royal Horticultural Society.

Idared (Group VI) was introduced in the United States in 1942 (see page 90), but not sent to England for trials until 1959. Its season in Britain is from November right through to March and it is best as a keeping dessert apple, picked as late as possible.

Merton Knave (Group VI) was raised by M. B. Crane at the John Innes Institution in 1948 from 'Laxton's Early Crimson' × 'Epicure' and put on trials from 1960. It was at first called 'Merton Ace', but renamed on its

Above: 'Idared'   Below: 'Discovery'

'Suntan'

of compact habit, perhaps a little slow to come fully into bearing but thereafter it never ceases to crop generously.

Suntan (Group VII) was raised in 1955 at East Malling Research Station by Dr Frank Alston from 'Cox's Orange Pippin' × 'Court Pendu Plat'. It went on trials in 1967 and was introduced in 1975, winning an Award of Merit in 1980. The apple's ground colour, which is green, turning golden-yellow, is flushed and striped orange-red with some grey-brown russetting. The flesh is pale yellow, coarse, juicy, acidic until fully ripe, perhaps at Christmas, and strongly aromatic. In season from late October to January, 'Suntan' is a triploid cultivar. The tree is vigorous, so it is usually advisable to have it on a dwarfing rootstock, and it makes spurs fairly freely.

Jonagold (Group VI) was raised in the United States (see page 90) and introduced to Britain in 1968. It is planted widely as a late storage variety for use from November to March. The fruit is large with a yellow ground flushed, mottled, and striped red, but sometimes poorly coloured. The flesh is white, crisp, and juicy, and of superb flavour. 'Jonagold' is, however, a triploid, although not over-vigorous, and for garden planting the very similar 'Falstaff', which is a diploid, might be a better choice.

Greensleeves (Group V) is another of Dr Frank Alston's raisings at East Malling, from 'James Grieve' × 'Golden Delicious' in 1966. On trial from 1972, it received an Award of Merit in 1981. The fruit is green, turning greeny-yellow when ripe, and the flesh is creamy-white, crisp, and juicy, with a pleasant and refreshing flavour. 'Greensleeves' has a long flowering period and is an excellent pollinator for many other apples, always setting a good crop itself, even in late-frost seasons. The tree is compact in habit and makes spurs readily, even on one-year wood after the second year; at the National Fruit Trials 'Greensleeves' gave twice as much fruit as 'Cox's Orange Pippin' over the first four fruiting years. Its season is from early October into November, coming between 'James Grieve' and 'Spartan'.

'Greensleeves'

Katy (Group VI) was raised in 1947 at Balsgard Fruit Breeding Institute, Sweden, from 'James Grieve' × 'Worcester Pearmain' and brought to England for trials in 1968. Called 'Katja' in its homeland, it was intended as a replacement for 'Worcester Pearmain' in orchards – it forms spurs more freely and in trials the production was four times greater. Apples are pale yellow, flushed almost overall bright scarlet, with smooth but rather tough skins and long stalks, in season September into early October, not keeping long. The fine-textured flesh is white and juicy with a pleasant flavour.

'Katy'

Jupiter (Group VII), also raised at East Malling by Dr Frank Alston, was from 'Cox's Orange Pippin' × 'Starking'. It has most attractive fruit with an orange-red flush and stripes on a greenish-yellow ground. The flesh is crisp, juicy, and of definite Cox flavour, worth keeping for eating in November, December, or later. 'Jupiter' is a strong rival to 'Cox's Orange Pippin' for garden planting – it is healthier, much less fussy about soil, yields a bigger crop, and produces apples with a longer storage life. Its main disadvantage is that it is a triploid and can make a big tree, but this ceases to be a difficulty if it is grafted on a dwarfing rootstock. Like other triploids it is no good as a pollinator, but where three or more apples can be planted this need not be a problem. It has not been popular with commercial growers, who are frightened off by its rather large apples – market research has convinced them that housewives prefer to get four dessert apples to the pound, rather than three or even two – but it is now well established as a good garden variety.

Norfolk Royal Russet (Group VIII) is a new apple that appeared as a sport on a tree of 'Norfolk Royal' in the garden of the Reverend C. E. Wright at Burnham Overy Staithe, Norfolk. He noticed, in 1972, that the apples on one branch were completely different from those on the rest of the tree – they were russetted all over, with a few speckles of light red on the sunny sides, and had a clean, dry finish, pleasing to the touch. 'Norfolk Royal' itself is a handsome dessert apple, usually almost completely flushed with scarlet,

'Norfolk Royal Russet'

but with an unattractively tough and greasy skin. The new variety was introduced by Highfield Nurseries in 1983. The tree is of medium vigour with a neat, fairly upright habit of growth; it has proved a reliable cropper on rootstock MM.106. The apple is crisp and firm with a distinctive rich, sweet flavour. Altogether 'Norfolk Royal Russet' is an excellent and exciting garden variety for eating off the tree in October and through to November when stored.

Bountiful (Group III) was raised at East Malling by Dr Frank Alston from 'Cox's Orange Pippin', open-pollinated on a Kent orchard. (The pollen parent was subsequently determined by Dr Alston to have been 'Lane's Prince Albert'.) It was the first new cooking apple to be raised since 'Howgate Wonder' over fifty years earlier and was introduced by Highfield Nurseries in 1984 only after lengthy trials had proved it to be an excellent garden variety, with several important advantages for the amateur grower over the popular 'Bramley's Seedling', with which it was in direct competition. 'Bountiful' is a very fertile, diploid variety, unlike 'Bramley's Seedling', which is a triploid with sterile pollen. The tree grows to only about half the size of 'Bramley's Seedling', starts to crop earlier in its life, and gives a much heavier yield in the first four years after planting. Its compact habit makes it exceptionally suitable for gardens where space is restricted and, because it forms spurs freely, 'Bountiful' is easy to grow as a cordon, unlike 'Bramley's Seedling'.

'Bountiful' apples are predominantly green with some orange-red stripes or patches. They are ready in October and keep into January in cool storage – when other apples have been eaten or are past their best in late winter 'Bountiful' is still good for eating as dessert. Used as a cooker, it needs very little added sugar, because of the sweetness it inherits from its seed parent.

Jester (Group VII) was raised in 1965 by Dr Frank Alston at East Malling, from 'Worcester Pearmain' × 'Starkspur Golden Delicious'. The apples are scarlet over a yellow-green ground, with a smooth and shiny skin; the flesh is very white, crisp, and juicy. To taste them at their best, pick them in mid-October when they are at the peak of colour and keep them in the cool for a week or so before eating. 'Jester' is a precocious variety with freely produced spurs and of compact habit but with wide branch angles, needing only minimum pruning. It sets heavily but thins naturally at June drop to one fruit per truss. It is a good pollinator at low temperatures, in particular for 'Cox's Orange Pippin', 'Jupiter', and 'Spartan'.

Redsleeves (Group VI) was raised by Dr Frank Alston at East Malling, from 'Exeter Cross' × an unnamed seedling TSR15T3, as part of a programme to breed in resistance to scab and mildew. Released in 1985, it is a healthy tree, compact and very fertile, which crops early in its life and needs very little pruning. 'Redsleeves' is a good pollinator for 'Cox's Orange Pippin' and produces lots of apples coloured red on yellow-green ground, often needing thinning for good sizes, which ripen in late August. The flesh is sweet, crisp, and juicy when ripe.

Fiesta (Group VII) was raised at East Malling by Dr Frank Alston in 1972 from 'Cox's Orange Pippin' × 'Idared' and given extensive trials on certain orchards and at the National Fruit Trials before being introduced by several nurseries in 1987, the year it received an Award of Merit. These trials do seem to have shown that this variety may well be the long-sought-after reliable alternative to 'Cox's Orange Pippin', particularly as it extends the season of Cox-type apples. The apple is evenly shaped with an attractive red blush and stripes on a yellow ground, without russetting, the skin finish being smooth but not greasy. It stores successfully into January or, in cool conditions, beyond. The flesh is very crisp and juicy with Cox-like flavour. 'Fiesta' fruits early in its life, as a trial over three years showed, when yields nearly twice those of 'Cox's Orange Pippin' were recorded. It is very fertile, setting fruit well at lower temperatures than does 'Cox's Orange Pippin'. It is a good pollinator, cross-pollinates successfully with many other apples, and is partly self-fertile.

Elstar (Group VII) is a variety new to Britain, although well known in Holland, where it was raised at Wageningen in about 1972 from 'Golden Delicious' × 'Ingrid Marie'. It is a round, thick-skinned apple, flushed half to overall with bright red on a yellow ground, that keeps well from October to January. The creamy-white flesh is highly flavoured, juicy, crisp, even hard.

Rubinette is another new apple only recently available in Britain. It was bred in Switzerland in 1966 by Walter Hauenstein-Roschli of Rafz, from 'Golden Delicious', believed to have been pollinated by 'Cox's Orange Pippin'. The fruit is described by the raiser as having a colour ranging from brilliant red stripes to pale shading on a yellow ground and the flesh as being yellowish, crisp, and juicy, with a delicious flavour that lingers on the palate. It can be eaten off the tree or kept in cool storage through to Christmas. 'Rubinette' has been ranked very high in tastings in Switzerland, both by experts and consumers, and those in Britain who have tried it seem to agree that the flavour is most unusual and enjoyable.

Falstaff is another apple only recently released. It was raised by Dr Frank Alston at East Malling from 'James Grieve' × 'Golden Delicious' as long ago as 1966 and was from the same cross and made at the same time as 'Greensleeves'. It was sent to the National Fruit Trials in 1972/3 but was overshadowed by 'Jonagold', which had arrived a little earlier. Arguably, though, it is superior to 'Jonagold' – it gives a much higher yield, usually about double, of apples of a smaller, more acceptable, size; it is less vigorous, being a diploid; and it is a good pollinator (which 'Jonagold' is not), especially for 'Cox's Orange Pippin'. Its parentage should guarantee it being a worthy garden tree. The oblong fruit bears red stripes on a yellow ground and has excellent skin finish. It is a crisp, very juicy apple, with a good acid-sugar balance, ready to eat in October but keeping well in cool storage to Christmas. As to flavour, it was the East Malling selection most popular among the staff, who are a hard bunch of people to please.

Ballerina, or Columnar, Apple Trees

The upright and narrow habit of these trees is inherited from 'Wijcik', a sport of 'McIntosh' discovered in British Columbia in 1964, which grows rather like a sturdy, natural cordon. The flowers and fruit are borne on short spurs at close intervals all up the single main stem, with few if any side branches. 'Wijcik' was crossed at East Malling with varieties of normal tree form, and when up to half the resulting

Ballerina apples growing at the Institute of Horticultural Research, East Malling, Kent

seedlings turned out to be columnar also it was decided to carry out a major breeding programme. Four selections of columnar trees, from crosses made in 1976, have been grafted on appropriate rootstocks and were released in the 1988/9 season.

Selections that combine their columnar habit with good fruit quality will make useful, easily manageable trees for the amateur, grown just like cordons but with less pruning required. Other selections with ornamental qualities such as red or double flowers, brightly coloured small fruits, or purple or cut-leaved foliage will have appeal as decorative garden features. Columnar trees could be planted at very close intervals to form a colourful and productive screen, or they could be planted in orchards as slimline pollinators, among a main variety such as 'Cox's Orange Pippin'. They are bred to be resistant to mildew. All in all, the columnars represent the most exciting new development in the fruit world for many years.

Maypole, from 'Wijcik' × 'Baskatong', is an ornamental crab apple with purple-tinted young leaves, carmine flowers in May, and purple-red fruits that can be made into jelly in September. It has very few side branches, which need minimal pruning; left alone it resembles in habit the ornamental cherry *Prunus* 'Amanogawa'. It should reach a height of about 10 ft (3 m) after six or seven years.

Bolero (Group IV), from 'Wijcik' × 'Greensleeves' is a dessert variety. Its apples are green with a golden blush, crisp, sweet, and juicy, and ready mid-September. Trees on trials have reached a height of 11 ft (3.4 m) in six years.

Polka (Group VI), from 'Golden Delicious' × 'Wijcik', has attractive blossom, followed by red and green dessert apples, crisp, juicy, and sweet, ready in late September. Judicious thinning is advised to prevent over-cropping and maintain fruit size. With minimal pruning it forms a natural cordon.

Waltz (Group VI), from 'Wijcik' × 'Golden Delicious', carries red and white blossom in mid-May, even flowering on one-year wood. Afterwards it bears predominantly crimson-on-green dessert apples; these are ready early in October but keep well in cool store round to May. Trees at East Malling reached a height of 9 ft 6 in (2.9 m) in six years.

Genetic Dwarf Apple Trees

A breakthrough in fruit-tree breeding is the recent arrival of the genetic dwarf, a tree whose genes control its size.

Goldilocks, the first such apple to reach Britain, was bred by Georges Delbard in France from 'Maigold' × 'Grive Rouge'. Grafted on MM.106 rootstock for a good root system, it makes a very small bush, only about 4 ft 6 in (1.4 m) in height at maturity. It bears large, green, dessert-quality apples with a tart and juicy flesh, ready to pick in late September or early October and keeping a few weeks in cool storage. 'Goldilocks' should be in demand for growing in tubs and very confined spaces and I am impressed by the first trees I have seen, well stocked with big apples. It flowers in mid-season along with many other apples, so cross-pollination is not likely to be a problem.

APPLES IN THE UNITED STATES OF AMERICA

The first orchards in Connecticut were planted by Dutchmen in about 1635 at Hartford, and by the 18th century varieties had become established that remained favourites for two hundred years or more. 'Black Gilliflower', an odd-shaped apple with a peculiar aroma but favoured for baking, 'Roxbury Russet', and 'Westfield-Seek-No-Further' were all distributed in due course around New England.

Settlers arriving in Novia Scotia from New England in 1761 found apple trees in bearing, probably first planted by earlier French immigrants, and by 1764 they were recorded as top-grafting the trees over to their preferred varieties. In the early part of the 19th century, however, fruit growing generally was still fairly primitive, with seedling trees outnumbering grafted varieties and orchards often neglected and depressing in their lack of fruitfulness.

John Chapman, an itinerant missionary famous in folklore as Johnny Appleseed, is said to have roamed the Ohio valley in the first years of the 19th century, planting apple seeds by streams and trails, and pruning the growing trees, for the benefit of Indians and pioneers. By 1845, the year of his death at the age of 71, he had established a string of apple-growing nurseries and orchards from Pennsylvania in the east through Ohio and into Indiana in the west. Presumably these seedlings must have been good mainly for cider fruit, but he encouraged the wide planting of apple trees and this helped the survival of frontiersmen.

Claimed to be the oldest apple tree in the Pacific Northwest is one planted in 1825 at Fort Vancouver on the Columbia River, Washington; it was grown from a seed brought from England by Lieutenant E. Simpson of the Hudson Bay Company. A photograph taken in 1916 showed it to be struggling to survive but it was taken in hand, pruned, sprayed, and fertilized, and when photographed again in 1971 it was flourishing and, furthermore, had been spared the threat of removal by builders of the Vancouver Freeway Project.

Californian varieties in 1850 included 'Rhode Island Greening', 'Roxbury Russet', 'Winesap', and 'Red Romanite', which had been brought over from New York State and planted in the Napa Valley. These were still popular in the years before World War I, as were 'Red Astrachan', 'Fall Pippin', 'Baldwin', 'Gravenstein', 'Northern Spy', 'Golden Russet', 'Westfield-Seek-No-Further', and 'Yellow Newtown' — all lovely names to roll off the tongue. Very few of them are now grown commercially and today stock for planting in home gardens can be hard to find.

To grow apples successfully in the United States it is necessary to choose the varieties that are best suited to the area in which you live, so that you grow worthwhile crops that, preferably, ripen when apples are in comparatively short supply in the stores. The crucial factor is winter chill — not only how much a variety can stand, but also how much it needs. Most apples need at least nine hundred hours of chill, with the temperature at 45° F (7° C) or lower, and some need as many as twelve hundred. Suitable proven varieties can, though, be found for most areas. Most varieties can be grown in hardiness zones 6 and 7 and some notably hardy ones succeed in zone 5 and parts of 4, but many regions in zones 8 and 9 can grow only a few select varieties that need little winter chill — around five hundred hours. The descriptions that follow give, in each case, the hardiness zone or zones for which the variety is recommended.

Early varieties
Akane (zones 5–7) is a Japanese hybrid, named in 1970, from 'Jonathan' × 'Worcester Pearmain'. The apples have a red skin and crisp, juicy, white flesh and are best eaten off the tree. 'Akane' is a light bearer, but healthier than its parent 'Jonathan', which has proved its worth in Canada.

Anna (zones 8, 9) originated in Israel and bears, heavily, its large green apples with red blush. For pollination, it must be near another early-flowering apple, such as 'Dorsett Golden' or 'Ein Shemer'.

Dorsett Golden (zones 8, 9) came from the Bahamas and is a dual-purpose variety, pollinating with 'Anna' or 'Ein Shemer'. It bears well its 'Golden Delicious'-type apples.

Ein Shemer (zones 8, 9) is another 'Golden Delicious'-type from Israel, pollinating with 'Anna' or 'Dorsett Golden'. It bears quite heavily.

Jersey Mac (zones 5–8) came from New Jersey in 1971 and is a 'McIntosh'-type ('New Jersey 24' × 'July Red'). It forms a vigorous tree and bears good quality red apples.

Lodi (zones 5–8) originated in 1924 at the New York State Experiment Station from 'Montgomery' × 'Yellow Transparent'. It can be a biennial bearer that needs thinning in its 'on' year. It has large, light green apples with orange blush, best used for cooking.

Tydeman's Early (zones 6–9) originated, as 'Tydeman's Early Worcester' (see page 81), in England. Its apples are almost entirely red from an early stage and all ripen together; it is probably best grown on a dwarfing rootstock to restrain its lanky growth.

Early to mid-season varieties
Gravenstein (zones 5–9) reached the United States from Germany via Britain in about 1760. A triploid variety, it makes a vigorous, spreading tree that bears large red apples with crisp and juicy, greenish flesh. Because it flowers very early it can be difficult to pollinate, needing two other trees – perhaps 'Winter Banana' and 'Red Astrachan'.

Jonamac (zones 5–8) originated in New York State from 'Jonathan' × 'McIntosh'. It is a heavy bearer of good-quality 'McIntosh'-type, but milder, apples. It is more disease-prone than its parents.

Liberty (zones 5–8), another from New York State, fruits abundantly with sweet and juicy apples, almost entirely red. It is a healthy variety, very resistant to diseases.

Paulared (zones 5–8), introduced in 1967 by Hilltop Nurseries, Michigan, is grown widely in the United States and Canada. Its red apples on yellow ground make good eating but can also be cooked, having a slightly tart flavour. It colours early but is best not picked until mature, as it hangs on well.

Prima (zones 6–8) originated in Illinois and has heavy crops of juicy red apples; their quality is fair but 'Prima' is valued chiefly for its resistance to disease. A vigorous, spreading tree, it thrives in the Midwest and near the northwest coast.

Mid-season varieties
Cortland (zones 4–8) crops heavily and is preferred by some home gardeners to 'McIntosh' as a dual-purpose apple. It has large, red-striped fruits with white flesh. It originated in New York State in 1915 and does well in the high west and the northeast, including Canada. 'Starkspur Cortland' is a dwarfer cultivar and there is also 'Early Cortland'.

Gala (zones 5–8), raised in New Zealand (see page 80), has done well in the United States as a quality dessert apple with a good storage life. The highly coloured mutant 'Royal Gala' is now also available in the United States.

Honeygold (zones 3–5) was raised at the University of Minnesota and named in 1969. It was bred from 'Golden Delicious' × 'Haralson' with cold winter areas in mind. Its long-keeping apples have yellowy-green skin and 'Golden Delicious' flavour, crisp and juicy.

Jonathan (zones 5–8) is widely grown commercially in the central United States, having originated with P. Rick, Woodstock, New York, before 1826. It has many clones but usually bears medium-sized, red-flushed, firm, and juicy apples. For the home garden, 'Akane' is sometimes preferred, or 'Stark Jon-A-Red'.

McIntosh (zones 4–7) originated in Dundas County, Ontario, soon after 1800 and was propagated from 1835 onwards; it is now well known and widely grown. Fruits are yellow with bright red flush, although maturing with less colour in warmer areas, and are quite large with sweet and juicy flesh. Trees grow vigorously, needing semi-dwarfing stocks in home gardens. There have been many descendants, including 'Empire', 'Jonamac', 'Tydeman's Red', and 'Spartan'.

Winter Pearmain (zones 5–10), of unknown origin but popular in southern California, bears large green apples of excellent quality. It takes about seven years to start fruiting, however, and is not happy in colder areas.

Mid-to-late-season varieties
Empire (zones 5–7) was raised in New York State and is another 'McIntosh' × 'Golden Delicious' cross. It has good quality fruits, uniformly red-striped, with crisp and juicy, cream-coloured flesh. It colours up early, so it is tempting to pick it before it has reached full maturity. Because it is a regular bearer and its apples store well, it may be preferable to 'McIntosh' for home gardens.

Delicious (zones 4–7) originated in Jesse Hiatt's orchard in Maddison County, Iowa, in the mid-1880s. Possibly a seedling from a nearby 'Yellow Belleflower' tree, it was named 'Hawkeye' by Hiatt. C. M. Stark pronounced it 'delicious' at a fruit show he sponsored in Louisiana and, when he bought the rights from Hiatt and introduced it in 1895, he changed the name to 'Delicious'. It soon became extremely popular – by the mid-1920s it was said to have seven or eight million offspring. The fruit is oblong-conical in shape, with five distinctive knobs on the end; the skin is red overall and the flesh sweet, crisp, and juicy. A biennial tendency can be controlled by thinning in the 'on' years.

Several sports have appeared from 'Delicious', the most famous being 'Red Delicious', which has replaced its parent in popularity in the United States and British Columbia, apples being found in every fruit store. Others are: 'Starkrimson Red Delicious'; a genetic dwarf, 'Starkspur Compact Red Delicious'; and the highly coloured 'Redchief'. Another, 'Starking', sported on a branch of 'Delicious' grown by Lewis Mood in Monroeville, New Jersey, in 1921. Stark Brothers judged it to be a true bud sport and purchased the branch for $6,000 (£1,500).

Golden Delicious (zones 5–9) originated as a chance seedling found by A. H. Mullins in Clay County, Virginia, in 1890. It may have been a seedling from 'Grimes Golden', pollinated by an old Virginian apple 'Golden Reinette'. It was introduced by Stark Brothers in 1916. At first considered simply as a good pollinator for 'Red Delicious', it was slow to become popular but, being a prolific and fertile variety, it is now the parent of many new cultivars growing all over the world. Because it bears heavily, even on young trees, it sometimes needs thinning. The apples are greenish-yellow with a pink flush when ripe, firm,

The blossom of 'Golden Delicious', showing the stamens and stigma against the pale petals

crisp, and juicy. 'Starkspur Golden Delicious' is a dwarf form. 'Smoothee' is a sport with less russet and a smoother skin.

Spartan (zones 6–9), named in 1936, was raised in Canada, at the Summerland Experiment Station, British Columbia, from 'McIntosh' × 'Yellow Newtown' and is now grown quite widely in the United States. The purplish-red apples, of medium size, have an attractive bloom; the flesh, which is very white, is crisp, juicy, and pleasantly aromatic. 'Spartan' crops quite heavily and often needs thinning, but, in dry summers, it needs regular watering if the fruits are to reach their full size. It is an excellent choice for growing in the home garden, particularly when it is on a dwarf rootstock.

Winter Banana (zones 7–9) was introduced by D. Florey in 1890, in Indiana, and bears beautiful apples with pale, waxy skins and pink blush; the flesh is tender with a tangy flavour and a pleasing aroma. It flowers very early and needs a pollinator such as 'Red Astrachan' or 'Gravenstein'. The apples keep to mid-winter.

The fruits of 'Golden Delicious'

Late-season varieties

Granny Smith (zones 7–8) was raised in Australia in about 1860 (see page 74). Apples have tough, glossy green skins and crisp, tart flesh, only ripening successfully in areas having a long growing season.

Idared (zones 6–8) was raised in 1935 by Leif Veiner at the Idaho Experiment Station from 'Jonathan' × 'Wagener' and introduced in 1942. It is an excellent keeper, with a smooth, shiny skin almost solidly red and firm white flesh. It is a cooker if taken early, but matures with keeping into a late-winter dessert apple. (See also page 81.)

Jonagold (zones 5–8) was raised at the New York State Experiment Station in 1943 from 'Golden Delicious' × 'Jonathan' and named in 1968. It has been acclaimed for its colour, size, and quality and quite widely grown commercially but is a triploid, needing careful pollination in home gardens.(See also page 83.)

Mutsu (zones 6–8), which was introduced to the United States in 1949, is the apple known as 'Crispin' in Britain. A triploid with sterile pollen, it is a vigorous grower unless grafted on a dwarfing rootstock. It bears large, oblong, greenish fruits, yellowish when ripe and with a purple flush, which keep very well in store, unless picked too ripe, and so are valuable for late-winter eating. The flesh is firm, crisp, and of excellent flavour.

Yellow Newtown (zones 5–9), raised at the New York State Experiment Station, makes a vigorous tree whose greeny-yellow, medium-sized apples have firm, crisp flesh. It is useful both for dessert and for pies but is a biennial bearer.

Northern Spy (zones 4–6) originated in Roswell Humphrey's orchard, East Bloomfield, New York, before 1840. It is slow to come into bearing, somewhat biennially, and probably best if grown on a semi-dwarfing rootstock to reduce this waiting period. The apples are large with yellow and red stripes and firm, crisp flesh. Excellent for dessert and for cooking, they keep well but bruise easily. Resistant to woolly aphids, it was used in the raising of rootstock MM.106.

Rome Beauty (zones 5–8) came from H. N. Gillett in Lawrence County, Ohio, before 1848, and is a heavy bearer from an early age of large, round, solid red apples that keep well. The texture is somewhat coarse, but firm and crisp, making it one of the best apples for baking. 'Red Rome' is one of several sports that have maintained the variety's popularity.

Roxbury Russet (zones 6–7) probably originated in Massachusetts, but as early as 1649 was taken to Connecticut and, later, to New York, Ohio, Indiana, and Michigan. A popular medium-sized russet apple that has for a very long time been a favourite winter apple for keeping, it is still planted in the northeast.

Stayman (zones 5–8), a sport of the popular variety 'Winesap', originated with J. Stayman of Leavenworth, Kansas, in 1866. It bears very late-maturing red apples with a tart, rich, winy flavour and firm, crisp flesh, probably better tasting than those of its parent and good both for dessert and cooking. The tree is of moderate vigour but not a pollinator for others. 'Staybrite', a triploid with sterile pollen, is a new, highly coloured sport.

Extra-hardy newcomers

The following extra-hardy cultivars, bred with cold-winter areas in mind, were raised at the University of Minnesota.

Red Baron, a mid-season variety, came from 'Golden Delicious' × 'Red Duchess'; its round, medium-sized red fruits have a tart flavour and are good both for dessert and in pies.

Regent is a late variety whose dessert-quality fruits keep well into winter; it has bright red skin and crisp, juicy flesh. The tree is vigorous.

PICKING AND STORING

Apples are easier to pick than pears, but even so need to be treated with care – once bruised, they soon begin to rot. Never pick an apple without its stalk, because this leaves a hole through which decay can quickly enter. And be careful not to pick too soon – an apple needs its full term on the tree to soak up the sun, build up its skin finish, develop its full flavour, and store away reserves, all of which will allow it to keep longer before being eaten.

Pick only when the apples are dry. Raise each one in the palm of the hand, turning it slightly; only if it comes away easily from the spur is it ready for picking. Take care not to tug off the spur, because, if you do, one or two of next year's fruit buds will be lost with it. You can avoid this by holding the thumbnail carefully against the stalk as you twist the apple. It is a good idea to 'pick over' a tree several times, especially with the early varieties, taking the ripest first from the sunnier side, rather than having too many in the house which go soft more quickly than they can be eaten.

The exact date to pick the later, keeping apples has to be a matter of experience with your particular cultivars in their particular environment. Trees on sandy soil ripen fruits sooner than those on heavy land. Trees growing in grass usually retain their fruits better than those in cultivated ground. The weather must dictate the decision, but harvest is near when the pips are turning brown and windfalls include otherwise undamaged apples. The imminent arrival of severe air frost makes harvesting essential.

Ideally, apples should be stored in a draught-free place such as a cellar or garden shed, away from bright light. They should be kept cool, preferably at under $45° F (7° C)$, and should not be subjected to fluctuations in temperature. I keep mine in shallow, slatted trays, standing them, not quite touching, on newspaper and putting rolls of paper between the rows. The trays are stacked in a simple 4 ft (1.2 m)-high cabinet. As apple-picking time coincides with mice and voles coming in to outbuildings I put down baited traps – having taken some trouble to get my fruit to this stage, I do not want it eaten by robbers. I label each tray with the name of the variety and the season for eating and examine fruits frequently in case any are rotting. I take apples into the house only a few at a time, because they soon deteriorate in the warmer conditions inside.

ROOTSTOCKS

Apples are grafted on to a range of rootstocks that control the rate at which the trees will grow as well as their eventual size. The most useful rootstocks for the home gardener are described here. The prefix M. denotes a rootstock that originated at East Malling Research Station, MM. one developed jointly by East Malling and the John Innes Horticultural Institution at Merton. After collaboration between East Malling and Long Ashton Research Station these stocks were re-issued free of known viruses, with 'EMLA' added.

M.27 is very dwarfing in its influence, producing trees unlikely to exceed 6 ft (1.8 m) in height or spread. These trees, which crop very early in life, are ideal for the smaller garden or for growing in tubs. They need little pruning, because they make comparatively small amounts of wood. As their root systems are small, they must be grown in fertile soil and kept staked.

M.9 is a dwarfing rootstock that makes trees some 7–8 ft (2.1–2.4 m) high. Again, because the root systems are small, trees must always be staked to prevent them falling over in high winds or when fully laden with apples. Trees on M.9 rootstock produce, early in life, fruit that is usually bigger and more highly coloured.

M.26, a semi-dwarfing rootstock, makes trees a little larger than those on M.9, of about 9–10 ft (2.7– 3.0 m), that need staking only on very exposed sites. For more vigorous growers like 'Bramley's Seedling' and for trees growing on 'strong' land it is preferable to MM.106.

MM.106 is the outstanding rootstock for garden planting where a more dwarfing M.9 or M.27 is unnecessary. It may be described as either semi-dwarfing or semi-vigorous, according to the soil in which it is planted. It forms a good anchorage and makes trees of 10–12 ft (3.0–3.7 m) in height and width, according to variety. MM.106 is free from suckering, crops more heavily than M.26, and is especially good on poor or sandy soils.

MM.111 is a vigorous rootstock used mainly for taller trees. It is suitable also for weak varieties grown on poor or very dry soil. The comparatively small range of apples grown on this rootstock is mainly sold as maiden (one-year-old) plants intended for growing on to make the taller trees.

Apple rootstocks and the approximate size of grafted trees after 10 years

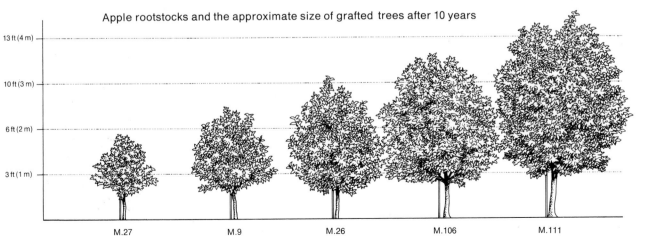

13 ft (4 m)
10 ft (3 m)
6 ft (2 m)
3 ft (1 m)

M.27   M.9   M.26   M.106   M.111

APRICOTS

Apricots (*Prunus armeniaca*) originated in China; they are mentioned in an account by the emperor Yü, traditionally the founder (*c*. 2205 BC) of the first Chinese dynasty. They still grow wild in the mountains near Peking. They must have been carried westwards by travellers along the silk route from China to the Caucasus because they were cultivated in Armenia very early on – Pliny the Elder (AD 23–79) calls them Armenian plums. Alexander the Great (356–323 BC) brought apricots to Greece and the ancient Egyptians grew them in large numbers for drying and for sale throughout Europe.

Apricots

APRICOTS IN BRITAIN

There seems to be no record of apricots growing in Britain before 1524, when John Wolf planted them in the grounds of Henry VIII's new Nonsuch Palace. Apricots were then mentioned in William Turner's *Newe Herball* of 1551, the name being spelt 'abrecock'. John Worlidge wrote in 1697 that fruits seldom matured except on trees grown against a wall but that apricots had recently been grown as dwarf trees, limited to a height of three feet (one metre), so that the fruits benefited from heat reflected off the earth.

Apricots flower in Britain in March and April while frosts are still likely, so they are best planted against a

sheltered wall over which a fine net or heavy-gauge polythene can be draped – taking care to keep it clear of the shoots carrying the blossom from the early-bud stage. The flowers are self-fertile, but a better set results from hand-pollinating with a fine brush – bees may dislike the weather at the time and not be working. It may be necessary to thin the fruitlets to give each apricot a fist's width in which to swell to full size. This is best done when they are about the size of walnuts. A net can be hung from above the tree to protect the fruits from birds.

The cultivar most usually grown nowadays, and probably the hardiest, is 'Moorpark', which was introduced by a famous English admiral, Lord Anson, in 1760. Anson engaged Capability Brown in 1753 to lay out the grounds at his home, Moor Park, near Watford, where he died, aged 65, two years after planting his apricot. By 1777, Richard Weston's nursery catalogue listed 'Moorpark' and half a dozen other varieties – 'Algiers', 'Breda', 'Brussels', 'Orange', 'Roman', and 'Turkey'. I suspect that these were grown under the protection of glass, which was then becoming popular.

Recommended varieties
Moorpark ripens its round, orange-yellow fruits with brown-red flush in late August. It is the variety most freely available, is well tried in most soils, and is recommended for outdoor planting. Because it can grow over-vigorously in its early years, it may have to be checked by root pruning. There is a clone called 'Early Moorpark' that ripens in early August but is otherwise similar.

Hemskirk was introduced by Lee of Hammersmith in 1820. It is larger than 'Moorpark' but otherwise similar and it ripens yellow fruits with red blotches in late July to August.

New Large Early, raised by Thomas Rivers in about 1873, ripens in late July and is the earliest apricot. Its oval, orange-yellow fruits are a little larger than 'Moorpark' and it is probably the best for indoor cultivation.

Farmingdale is a less vigorous variety from the United States that is said to be less susceptible to dieback. It bears medium-sized fruits, which are ready in July or August.

Alfred, another import from the United States, also ripens July–August and is also said to be resistant to dieback. Its crop of medium-sized fruits needs thinning to prevent it becoming biennial.

APRICOTS IN THE UNITED STATES OF AMERICA

The Spaniards took the apricot to the New World with the earliest settlements and the English established it in Virginia – the colonist and adventurer John Smith reported in 1629 that apricots were thriving there. Named varieties arrived in the United States before 1860, among the first being 'Moorpark' and 'Blenheim' (which became known as 'Royal'), both from England. Apricots are now grown commercially in large numbers in California, which enjoys a virtual world monopoly in canned and dried fruits. They are more winter hardy than other stone fruits, though, and can be grown in home gardens in many other parts, particularly the Atlantic states. Trees should not be planted in low-lying frost pockets and protection must be given from spring frosts.

Most apricots are self-fertile although brush-pollinating will ensure a better set. Because the fruits do not travel well they are not plentiful in stores and they are, in any case, far tastier when they are enjoyed fresh from the garden.

Recommended varieties
Chinese (zones 5–6) – also known as 'Mormon', from its origins in Utah – is a good choice for colder, western regions and mountainous areas, because it flowers late so that the blossom tends to miss unwelcome frosts. Trees bear heavy crops of small but sweet and juicy fruit at an early age.

Flora Gold (zones 5–8), which originated in California, is a genetic dwarf that grows naturally to only about half the size of most apricot trees. It ripens a heavy crop of early-season full-sized fruits.

Goldcot (zones 4–9), bred at the Michigan Experiment Station, flowers late and is extra hardy, bearing heavily in early to mid-season. Its medium-sized fruits are tough-skinned but tasty.

Harcot (zones 5–8) was bred in Ontario and is a cold-hardy variety that flowers late but matures early. It makes a heavy-bearing, quite compact, disease-resistant tree.

Moorpark (zones 5–7) has adapted well to the United States and is highly regarded. It tends to ripen unevenly, but this can be an advantage to the home gardener because it allows several pickings. The large fruit is orange with a deep blush, often dotted with brown and red.

Royal (zones 6–8) is a standard commercial variety in California, but it dislikes excessive heat – over 90° F (32° C) – at harvest time. It bears heavily in mid-season.

Royal Rosa (zones 6–8), which originated in California, ripens a little later than 'Moorpark'. It is of fairly compact habit and bears bright yellow, firm-fleshed, and aromatic fruit, sweet yet with a tart tang. For fruit eaten off the tree it is probably America's outstanding cultivar.

Scout (zones 4–6) came to the United States from Manchuria, via Canada. It makes a tall, vigorous, but upright tree bearing medium-sized, bronze-coloured fruits, somewhat flattened and ripening late.

CULTIVATION

Like other stone fruits, apricots appreciate a mulch of compost or well-rotted manure each year and a top dressing of sulphate of potash in late winter with lime added if necessary. If growth has been poor, apply nitrogen in spring and again in summer. While the fruits are swelling it is important to soak the feeding roots generously, remembering that wall-grown plants are vulnerable to drought because the wall and foundation soak up so much of any rain that falls. Lack of moisture can cause fruitlets to drop alarmingly and is also believed to be the main cause of dieback. Poor drainage, which leads to rotting of the roots in over-wet conditions, can also cause dieback.

Pruning should be done soon after harvesting – not in winter, when it can lead to fungal attack or dieback – and at the same time shoots needed to fill up spaces should be tied into position, while they are still pliable. Apricots fruit on shoots made the previous summer and also on naturally produced spurs off older wood, so summer pruning can induce more spurs – pinch out the tips of laterals when they are about 3 in (7.5 cm) long.

Trees can be bought as one-year-old, unpruned maidens or as ready-trained fans. In Britain they are normally grafted on St Julien A rootstock, the least vigorous available; in the United States the usual rootstock is the Manchurian hardy apricot.

In colder areas apricots may have to be grown in greenhouses. Outside, a wall space about 15 ft (4.5 m) wide and at least 6 ft (2 m) high should be allowed for the spread of a fan-trained tree. Trees that can be kept growing well in early summer are less attractive to aphids, which dislike sucking sap that is flowing strongly. If you do notice them on the foliage use a systemic spray.

Apricots do not keep long. They are best enjoyed as soon as they ripen, when they are full of flavour, although some people prefer them a little crisper, picked a day or two earlier. They should be picked with the stalk intact.

CHERRIES

Cherries appear to have originated in the area around the Dardanelles where Europe and Asia meet. The sweet cherries, *Prunus avium*, reached Britain and western continental Europe in prehistoric times. Their pits have been found in the remains of central European cave dwellings and show that cherries were gathered and used there in the Stone Age. The sour, or pie, cherry, *P. cerasus*, seems, though, to have spread more slowly. Theophrastus described the trees and the fruit in about 300 BC. By the 1st century BC, cherries were in cultivation in Italy – the Roman scholar-soldier Varro, in his book on farming written in about 50 BC, describes how cherries are grafted.

CHERRIES IN BRITAIN

It was the Romans who introduced the cultivated cherry to Britain. Pliny the Elder reported cherry trees being imported to Britain as early as AD 46 and the historian Tacitus reported in AD 79 that British soil produced good cherry crops. We may assume that the Romans planted trees in Kent and transported their cherries by sea and river to London.

There are few references to cherries between the departure of the Romans and the 14th century, when we know they were hawked through London streets. Unlike most other fruits, cherries do not continue to ripen after harvesting, so they have to be picked when ready and transported, sold, and eaten within four or five days. These early mentions must, then, refer to fruit grown close to London, probably in Kent.

The first named varieties seem to have appeared in the 16th century, but the history of the modern cultivated cherry can be said to have started with the experiments carried out early in the 19th century by Thomas Andrew Knight, who systematically hybridized and cross-pollinated cherries to produce commercial varieties that soon became well known in Britain. The Royal Horticultural Society listed 246 named cherries as being grown in its collection at Chiswick in 1827.

More recently, a sweet-cherry breeding programme was begun at the John Innes Horticultural Institution in the 1920s, using as parents some of the best commercial varieties. After lengthy trials, interrupted by World War II, the resulting cultivars were introduced in 1947. The John Innes Institution also co-operated with the Summerland Experiment Station in British Columbia, Canada, which has been responsible for the introduction of valuable new cultivars that have proved to be successful in Britain.

Recommended varieties

Choosing suitable cherries to plant in a garden can be a rather complicated affair, because most are self-sterile and so need pollinating by another cherry in flower at the same time, but this is not so easy to achieve, because many varieties are incompatible with each other or flower at dates which do not overlap. Reference to the Flowering Table on page 151 is necessary before choosing which cherries to plant, especially where there is room for several trees. Happily, a few self-fertile cultivars, more suitable for small gardens, have been developed in recent years.

The cultivars suggested here for garden planting are described in approximate order of ripening.

Sweet cherries

Early Rivers was introduced by Thomas Rivers in 1872 from seed of 'Early Purple Guigne'. It is among the first to flower and has large black cherries of good flavour, with red flesh and coloured juice, that usually ripen in mid-June; it is a reliable and heavy cropper, fairly vigorous, with a spreading habit.

Mermat is a promising new cultivar, raised at the John Innes Institution, which ripens its large black fruits in late June. It has inbred resistance to canker and has done well in trials.

Merchant, another promising introduction from the John Innes Institution, bears heavy crops of good-sized black fruits of top quality early in July. It has inbred resistance to bacterial canker and is useful as a donor for other cherries flowering at the same time.

Roundel Heart (or 'Roundel'), an old favourite not now often found, ripens in early July its large, heart-shaped, dark red fruits; they are sweet and juicy with white flesh. It is of moderate vigour, with an upright habit and healthy growth.

Merton Bigarreau – is like all varieties with 'Merton' in their names – a John Innes cultivar. 'Merton

'Merton Glory'

Bigarreau' is bred from 'Knight's Early Black' × 'Napoleon'. It makes a fairly vigorous tree that crops heavily, bearing good quality black cherries with coloured juice that ripen in the first half of July.

Merton Glory, also for late June or early July, has large yellow fruits with crimson flush and white juice. An outstanding variety, it is another universal donor.

Merton Favourite, produced from 'Knight's Early Black' × 'Schrecken', crops heavily with rich, sweet, dark crimson cherries with coloured juice in the second half of July. It has strong but compact growth.

Noir de Guben flowers very early and ripens its large, mahogany-coloured, red-juiced fruits in mid-July. It has vigorous, upright growth and is another universal donor.

Napoleon Bigarreau has large heart-shaped yellow cherries, with red flush and white juice, that ripen in mid- to late July. It crops well with a long season. Growth is weaker than most and it can get canker in poorly drained or heavy soil.

Van came from British Columbia and has proved an excellent choice for Britain; its bright red, shiny cherries ripen in mid- to late July and have sweet, red flesh. It is a vigorous tree of upright habit.

Bigarreau Gaucher has large, sweet, black cherries with dark flesh of high quality. It is valuable as a late variety; it ripens in mid- to late July and hangs on well. Growth is strong but fairly upright.

Stella was introduced to Britain from Summerlands Research Station in British Columbia and quickly won a First Class Certificate from the Royal Horticultural Society. It is resistant to bacterial canker and crops well and regularly, the large, dark red fruits ripening in late July. It is self-fertile.

Compact Stella is an irradiation-induced mutation or sport of 'Stella' from Summerland Experiment Station. It is noticeably shorter and narrower in habit than 'Stella', the buds being closer together along the more upright branches. Its fruits are exactly like those of 'Stella' and, like 'Stella', it is self-fertile. Until nurserymen get a really dwarf rootstock on which to graft cherries, 'Compact Stella' on 'Colt' rootstock is the best choice for planting alone in a confined space or in a tub.

Bradbourne Black is another late cherry for the end of July. The heart-shaped fruits are mahogany-skinned, with dark flesh and coloured juice. The tree, which flowers late, is at first upright and then spreading in habit.

Sunburst is a very new introduction, also from British Columbia; it is a self-fertile sweet cherry, similar to 'Stella' but having larger, crack-resistant, black fruits that ripen in late July. Its May flowers often miss the late frosts.

Lapins is a new, self-fertile Canadian cultivar. The fruits, which are extra large, have dark red, crack-resistant skins and are ready to pick in late July/early August.

Summit, recently arrived from Canada, crops in late July and bears dark red cherries. It is self-sterile.

Sour and Duke cherries
Morello, the only sour cherry to be recommended for gardens, is quite vigorous when young but never makes more than a small, round, and drooping head. It is self-fertile, and, flowering late itself, can also pollinate late-flowering sweet cherries. The fruits, which often hang in pairs or threes, ripen, turning a bright, shiny red, during August and into September when wall-trained. The ripe flesh is red, soft, juicy, and sharp but not acid. A 'Morello' cherry provides an admirable solution to the problem of what to plant on a north-facing wall; it positively enjoys this aspect and in April covers itself in foaming white blossom.

'Morello' now has a rival in 'Nabella', a heavy-cropping cultivar from Germany; of compact growth, it carries black fruits.

'Morello'

May Duke is the only representative worth considering for the garden of the group of Duke cherries, which probably originated as the result of crossing sweet and sour varieties. 'May Duke' is only partially self-fertile, but it pollinates sweet cherries. Its red fruits, which ripen in early July, have dark flesh and juice, and are soft and subacid, the taste being halfway between sweet and sour. Dukes are no longer in demand these days – they have been found to be unreliable in their cropping and rather susceptible to bacterial canker.

CHERRIES IN THE UNITED STATES OF AMERICA

Some cherries were being grown in North America very soon after the first settlements. The Red Kentish cherry was being cultivated in Massachusetts in 1629, only nine years after the Pilgrims had landed. By the middle of the 17th century cherries were widely distributed through the colonies and they advanced westwards with the settlement of the country. The story of George Washington, the hatchet, and the cherry tree is, of course, apocryphal but perhaps demonstrates that, by the time it was told, in 1806, a cherry tree in a Virginia garden could be taken for granted. By the mid-19th century the commercial production of cherries had begun and many new cultivars were introduced. Some were imported from England, but many, like 'Governor Wood', raised in Cleveland in 1842 and named after the state governor, Reuben Wood, originated in the United States.

Sweet cherries grow successfully in home gardens throughout the western states, except in southern California, the southwest desert, and in the higher mountains. East of the Rockies zone 6 is ideal, but cherries will grow in nearly every state north and northeast of Texas, except Minnesota and the Dakotas, in zones 5–7 and 9. Ideally, they like long, dry summers and chilly but not bitter winters. Sour cherries are rather hardier and may be safer around the Great Lakes, in most of New England, and much of the Great Plains.

Recommended varieties

Angela (zones 5–9), from Utah, is a sturdy, easy-to-manage tree that bears large, dark, crack-resistant cherries in late season. 'Emperor Francis' pollinates.

Bing (zones 5–9) is a standard commercial variety from Oregon producing in mid-season deep mahogany-red, juicy cherries. It needs a pollinator such as 'Black Tartarian' or 'Van'. Home gardeners will be more interested in the genetic dwarf version, 'Garden Bing', which originated in California. This self-fertile cultivar grows to 8 ft (2.4 m) or less in open ground and to only a few feet in a container.

Black Tartarian (zones 5–9) also originated in California and is an erect, vigorous tree that fruits early and heavily with sweet, black, medium-sized cherries, unfortunately somewhat prone to cracking. It is popular as a generous pollinator for most sweet varieties, including 'Bing' and 'Van'.

Emperor Francis (zones 5–7) fruits in mid-season with large yellow, blushed-red cherries – sweet and firm, they retain their flavour if preserved or cooked. 'Rainier' and 'Angela' are pollinators.

English Morello (zones 5–8), the 'Morello' so popular in Britain for north-facing walls (see page 96), grows happily in the northern United States, where it ripens late. The tree has rather weeping branches and is smaller than the sweet varieties, but easy to train.

Lapins (zones 5–7) from Summerland Experiment Station, British Columbia, is now becoming available in the United States. It is a self-fertile, sweet cherry with dark red, crack-resistant, and firm-textured fruit, ripening in late season. It is bound to become popular as an alternative to 'Stella'. (See also page 96.)

Montmorency (zones 5–9), of French origin, is probably the standard sour cherry both for commercial and home planting. The large red fruits have firm yellow flesh and crack-resistant skins, ripening in mid- to late season. It is self-fertile.

Rainier (zones 5–9) originated in Washington and is very hardy, vigorous, and productive. The large, blushed-yellow cherries resist cracking and have firm, juicy flesh, ripening in early to mid-season. Pollinators are 'Bing' and 'Van'.

Stark Gold (zones 5–8) is a sweet yellow cherry, whose fruits birds seem to ignore. It has survived winter temperatures of −30°F (−34°C) and still cropped heavily. It ripens early and bears crack-resistant fruit. It is a very good pollinator, needing one itself; most sweet varieties serve.

Stella (zones 5–9), the first true self-fertile sweet cherry, now very popular in England, originated in British Columbia. It bears early in life its dark red fruits and pollinates most other sweet cherries. (See also page 96.)

Summit (zones 5–8), another new cherry raised in British Columbia, has very large, sweet, black fruits early in the season. It needs a pollinator.

Van (zones 5–9), which is also popular in Britain (see page 96), has large, dark red cherries. It is very hardy and, as it can over-set its fruit, it will bear a crop even in borderline areas. It pollinates with 'Stella', 'Bing', and most others.

Windsor (zones 5–7) was raised by James Dougall of Windsor, Ontario, Canada, and introduced in 1881. It is probably the standard late, dark red, commercial cherry in the eastern United States; it usually bears a good crop in mid-season, even in borderline areas. It pollinates with 'Stella' or 'Angela'.

ROOTSTOCKS

Cherry growers have had to contend over the years with the difficulty of preventing birds from stripping the crop and the problem of having to climb high in the tree to harvest the fruit. The commonly used rootstock F.12/1 produced trees far too big for most gardens. What growers awaited was a dwarf rootstock to produce smaller trees, so that netting against birds would be easier and the long ladders used for fruit picking could be thrown away. The arrival in 1958 of a new rootstock for both fruiting and ornamental cherries was therefore enthusiastically welcomed.

The newcomer was 'Colt', a hybrid from a cross between *Prunus avium* and *P. pseudocerasus*, raised at East Malling Research Station. Growers quickly abandoned all seedling rootstocks with their variable vigour and habit and turned exclusively to 'Colt'. But, sadly, 'Colt' proved to be less dwarfing in its influence than expected – it produces trees about two-thirds the

'Stella'

size of those on F.12/1 – although it does produce trees that are healthy, resistant to bacterial canker, and easy to propagate and that fruit earlier in life than those on older rootstocks.

So the search goes on for a truly dwarfing rootstock that will do for cherries what M.9 or M.27 has done for apples and 'Pixy' for plums. In the United States researchers are working to improve on 'Mazzard' and 'Mahaleb', which have been popular rootstocks for many years. Meanwhile, the Belgian Research Station at Grand-Manil has bred a stock named 'Inmil' (code GM.9), which is a selection from a cross between *P. incisa* and a *P. serrula* hybrid. Trees on this stock grow to a height of no more than 6 ft (1 m) and reach full bearing in their fifth year. It is early days yet, though, to recommend this without qualification to the home gardener.

CULTIVATION

Cherries will thrive in a well-drained, fertile soil; a shallow or badly drained soil is likely to lead to disease or death. Sweet cherries produce their fruit buds near the base of the young lateral branches formed the previous summer and on older wood. Pruning should

be done only in spring, when wounds heal quickly, or fungal disease may enter the wound. Growing tips should be pinched out when the new shoots have made five or six leaves.

The sour cherry 'Morello' fruits almost entirely on growths made in the previous summer and so needs slightly different pruning. New shoots are thinned out in early summer to about 4 in (10 cm) apart, leaving one replacement shoot at the base of each fruit-carrying lateral. Do not pinch out growing tips, leave them to extend where there is room.

If it seems necessary, spring is also the time to apply a general fertilizer over the root area. Remember to water the roots as the fruits swell, particularly if the tree is planted against a wall. A wall gives off reflected warmth to ripen the fruits and also makes it easier to net the tree against birds, but it and its foundations soak up a lot of moisture.

At harvest time, it is best to pick over the tree several times as the cherries ripen. Always leave the stalks intact on the fruit.

Cherries suffer from few pests, the most destructive being birds, which attack both buds and ripening fruits. Aphids, black fly in particular, and sometimes caterpillars of the winter moth, attack young growth. Silver leaf and bacterial canker are the principal diseases. Grease-banding in autumn is worthwhile.

FIGS

A native of Asia Minor, the fig (*Ficus carica*) grows wild in the lands around the Mediterranean, to as far west as the Canary Islands. It has been well known since very early times. The harvesting of the fruit is shown in a wall painting in an Egyptian grave of the 12th Dynasty, some 2,000 years before Christ. The ancient Greeks prized and knew figs – Aristotle, in the 4th century BC, noticed that insects had to visit the young fruits, or they would drop off. In Italy, Cato the Elder, in about 200 BC, described six varieties and, by the 1st century BC, Pliny the Elder knew of twenty-nine varieties.

A fig tree, unfruitful because of unrestricted root growth

FIGS IN BRITAIN

Figs were included in the diet of the Romans in Britain – fig seeds have been found on several Roman sites – and the dried fruit formed part of army rations. That figs continued to be eaten in Britain after the Romans left cannot be doubted, but we have records of fig trees being grown only in the 16th century. John Claudius Loudon, a notable horticultural writer of the early 19th century and founder and first editor of *The Gardener's Magazine*, repeated a long-held tradition that Reginald Pole, Henry VIII's cardinal and, later, enemy, brought back from Rome a 'White Marseilles' fig tree that he planted at Lambeth Palace in 1525. By 1548, William

Turner was able to note in his *The names of herbs . . .* that there were 'divers fig trees in England in gardens'. In 1708, according to Henry Wise, gardener to Queen Anne, eight varieties of figs grew in the gardens of Hampton Court, Windsor, and Blenheim. Loudon, writing in 1834, described an orchard in Sussex of one hundred trees, each yielding every day a dozen figs the size of apples for sale in nearby watering places. He may have been referring to the fig garden at Bishop's Garth, West Tarring, in Sussex, which dates from 1745.

Cultivated varieties of the fig are self-fertile; they do not rely on insects for pollination. Their flowers are borne within the fleshy fruitlet and are of three types — male, female, and neuter. Embryo figs, about the size of peas, appear near the tips of the shoots in the leaf axils in August and September. In the following summer these embryo figs swell to maturity and a second crop appears beyond them on the shoots, but these never ripen and may even fall off. They should, in any case,

A fig tree, root-restricted and carefully trained

be removed so that the tree's energies are directed into fruits it *can* ripen. Then, near the tips of the branches, from six to ten embryo figs appear ready for next year.

In warmer climes all three crops will ripen. In Britain this is only possible under glass and at a high cost for heating, although the back wall of a conservatory attached to a house might well support a fig that could crop more than once.

An outdoor fig needs to be planted in a sun trap and must have its roots restricted if it is to produce fruit. The usual method of restricting the roots is to construct an open-based trough 2 ft (60 cm) long, wide, and deep, with its top 1 in (2.5 cm) above soil level. The sides may be made of paving slabs or bricks; the bottom should be packed with broken bricks or lumpy chalk or rubble to prevent tap roots from forming. The trough should then be filled with a mixture of good loam and fine mortar-rubble with a few handfuls of bonemeal. A plant grown against a wall and provided with this accommodation for its roots will need a wall space at least 7 ft (2 m) high by 10 ft (3 m) wide.

It is also possible to grow a fig in a 12 in (30 cm) pot. This could yield eight or more fruits a year, perhaps more if it is brought in under cover for the coldest part of the year. A fig in a pot in a conservatory is another possibility.

Whichever way you decide to grow your fig tree it is best to start with a well-rooted pot-grown plant; if planted in autumn it may need protection from frosts during the first winter. Plant about 1 ft (30 cm) away from the wall, with the roots teased out and spread in the hole, fill with soil and water in. Prune the shoots after planting, or in the spring, to encourage new ones to form for training fan-wise as they extend in summer. Because the roots are restricted, it is essential to water during dry spells, especially while the fruits are swelling. Figs are propagated from cuttings or layers, not by grafting, so are on their own roots; shoots that arise from below ground are not therefore suckers.

To encourage a good supply of frost-resistant, stubby wood that will carry the embryo figs through the winter, the growing points of the new shoots should be pruned in early July to about five leaves.

In late April, as new growth is starting, winter protection should be removed, any damaged wood pruned away, and the branches trained out against the wall. If there is surplus wood, then the branches to retain are those with the best supply of embryo figs showing; the others should be shortened to encourage new wood to branch out.

The fig is conveniently free of pests and diseases. It needs to be protected from birds and wasps, which attack the fruits just as they swell and colour up. Young shoots, especially if over-crowded, can get a grey mould on them in very wet seasons, and this, or any sign of canker, is best pruned away when noticed. The tips of the young shoots and the embryo figs should be protected against frost through the winter, easily done by wrapping them loosely in bracken or straw and removing this in late March; a dressing of general fertilizer over the rooting area and a mulching at the same time will prove beneficial.

Recommended varieties

The fruit is ready for gathering when a drop of nectar appears at the eye or when the side has split slightly under the pressure of juice inside. Figs gathered too early taste dry and woolly. Rich and juicy, freshly picked from your own tree in late summer, they are delicious.

There are five varieties commonly available in Britain that will allow you to enjoy this experience.

Brown Turkey is the variety most commonly grown; best for outdoor planting, it can also be grown in a greenhouse. Its large, pear-shaped figs, which ripen from late August, have chocolate-coloured skins and rich and juicy red flesh.

Brunswick has very large leaves as well as very large fruits with pale purplish-green skin and pink-tinged flesh, fairly rich and sweet, and ripening in mid- to late August. It is hardy outdoors in the south of England.

White Marseilles has rounder fruits with pale yellowish-green, almost opalescent, skin, slightly ribbed; the flesh is sweet, rich, and juicy, almost translucent. 'White Marseilles' ripens from mid-August, depending on situation, and is a somewhat shy bearer that needs, if not a conservatory, a well-protected and sunny position outdoors.

St Johns is a good variety for growing in pots because of its naturally dwarf habit; it is an earlier variety, hardly suitable for outdoors, that produces white-fleshed, pear-shaped fruits of good size.

White Ischia, another fairly dwarf variety, is a tremendous cropper of small, greeny-white figs with juicy, purplish flesh.

FIGS IN THE UNITED STATES OF AMERICA

The Spaniards brought figs to America. Varieties were sent from Spain to Hispaniola in 1520 and were reported to be bearing well in 1526. Figs were established in Florida before the end of the 16th century and, in 1629, John Smith recorded that Mistress Pearce, a settler at Jamestown, Virginia, harvested 'neere a hundred bushels of excellent figges'.

The first fig to reach California was planted in the garden of the mission at San Diego, probably as soon as the mission was established, in 1769. It was the variety now called 'Mission'.

The warmer parts of the United States around the west and southeast coasts suit the fig best and it grows contentedly, too, in the milder parts of the northeast and northwest, mainly in zones 10, 9, and, less certainly, 8.

The first crop each year blooms on the wood made the previous season and the second crop in late summer comes on new wood of the current year's growth. Over-heavy pruning or cold winter weather may eliminate the first crop, but the second will usually mature satisfactorily. In warmer districts both crops succeed, the second often being lighter.

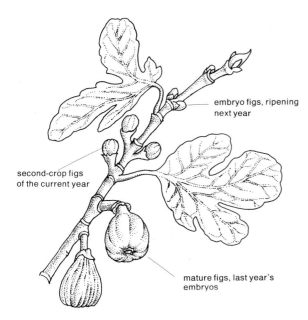

embryo figs, ripening next year

second-crop figs of the current year

mature figs, last year's embryos

Fruiting of figs

If a home-garden fig tree is making a foot or so (about 30 cm) of extension growth a year no fertilizer should be needed; if less, then a balanced feed can be applied. In Florida, for instance, where it may be necessary to counter the leaching by rain of soil nutrients, a light feed at monthly intervals may be necessary. Nitrogen dressing should not be over-done as this tends only to encourage unwanted lush growth.

Recommended varieties

The cultivars here recommended for home gardens in the United States are all self-fertile.

Brown Turkey (also called 'Black Spanish', 'Negro Largo', or 'San Piero') is a variety also widely grown in Britain (see page 102). The clone popular in California probably came from the Mediterranean via Mexico; it bears large fruits with violet-brown skins and pink flesh. The clone popular in the eastern states may have come from Italy via England; it is the most suitable fig for cold-winter districts – it can be grown in containers and brought under cover as necessary for its protection.

Celeste is believed to have originated in Malta and is also called 'Sugar' or 'Malta'. It has smaller, bluey-brown fruits whose flesh is more of an amber colour. It is hardy, and a favourite in the southeast and southwest.

Magnolia, also called 'Madonna', is the variety known as 'Brunswick' in Britain. It thrives in the southeastern states and carries large yellowy-green figs with pinkish flesh.

Mission still thrives in the southwest and does well, too, in the warmer areas of the southeast. The fruits are almost black, with deep red flesh.

MEDLARS

Medlar trees are indigenous to southeast Europe and Asia Minor and were certainly grown by the ancient Greeks, whose name for the genus – made up from 'mesos', a half, and 'pilos', a ball – neatly describes the fruit. The specific name, *Mespilus germanica*, implies that it became naturalized in central Europe and the fruits are known to have been eaten, though not necessarily grown, by the Romans in Britain.

Chaucer referred to 'the fairest Medlar tree that ever yet in all my life I sie', and medlars are recorded as being in cultivation in Britain by the early 16th century. William Turner, in 1540, notes them as being common in England. Certainly Shakespeare was familiar with them; in *As You Like It* Rosalind says to Touchstone 'I'll graft it with you, and then I shall graft it with a medlar; then it will be the earliest fruit i' th' country, for you'll be rotten ere you be half-ripe, and

Medlars in autumn

that's the right virtue of the medlar'. Seeds or trees are believed to have been taken to America by French Jesuits; in Florida they are now sometimes used as hedgeplants, having escaped to the semi-wild.

At one time medlar trees were grown in the gardens of almost every property of consequence in Britain, for their decorative value as much as for their fruits – they offer a fine display of big white flowers in late May and early June. The flowers are self-fertile and have large, leaf-like, pointed sepals. After pollination, the flowers swell into the unique fruits, which ripen, as the leaves change colour in autumn, into knobbly, brown spheres with their sepals still attached.

Recommended varieties

Nottingham, sometimes called the common medlar, is the cultivar most often grown and is usually considered the best flavoured. It makes a flat-topped little tree, growing slowly to no more than 12–15 ft (3.5–4.5 m) in height and rather less in width, that lives to a healthy old age. The branches sometimes turn suddenly at right-angles to give a somewhat contorted but 'architectural' shape. The leaves are large and handsome, downy and dull green in summer but turning to fine autumn tints of yellow, pink, and brown before falling in November. The fruits are about $1\frac{1}{2}$ in (4 cm) in diameter.

Dutch, also called 'Monstrous', has a much bigger and more spreading weeping habit, and it produces, though less prolifically, larger fruits, whose flavour is usually considered less good.

Royal was introduced from France in 1860 and it crops heavily, even when quite young, with medium-sized fruits of good flavour. It has a fairly upright habit and makes a larger tree than 'Nottingham'.

CULTIVATION

Medlars used to be grafted on to hawthorn as the rootstock, but Quince A is used nowadays, keeping the trees to a moderate size suitable for the garden. Seedling trees are not recommended – they do not come true and take longer to start fruiting. The tree is best planted against a stake and so trimmed as to produce a clear stem at least 3 ft (1 m) tall before the

Above: 'Nottingham'   Below: 'Dutch' after leaf fall

head is allowed to branch out. Almost any soil is suitable except one that is waterlogged and, once planted, a medlar is remarkably trouble free. Regular cropping is more certain if the tree can be planted in a position out of cold winds at blossom time; and in cooler districts this is important.

When ripe in autumn the fruits are brown and hard, looking rather like small russet apples. They should be left on the tree until frosts seem likely and picked on a dry day. They must then be 'bletted' – stored, stalks upward, on a bed of dry sand or straw in a frost-free place for two to three weeks, until the flesh turns brown and buttery and the fruits become edible, in a condition best described as incipient decay. Dipping the ends of the stalks in a solution of table salt prevents the fruits from rotting during the bletting process.

Medlars need little pruning, no more than thinning to keep the head shapely and open to let in light and the removal of any dead wood. Initial shaping is done exactly as for half-standard apples and the fruits form on the two-year wood in the same way. Medlar leaves sometimes show dark blotches between the veins that herald the appearance of a white mould; the disease is best controlled by picking off the affected leaves for burning. Leaf-eating caterpillars might appear, as on almost any fruit tree, and are controlled by picking off as soon as noticed or by applying a suitable spray.

MULBERRIES

Pliny the Elder described the mulberry as the wisest of trees because it awaits the end of cold weather before bursting into leaf and is the first to shed its leaves in autumn. He was referring to the black mulberry (*Morus nigra*), which probably originated in the southern part of the Caucasus and was carried westwards into the lands of the Bible. This is the species that has for a very long time been cultivated in many parts of Europe. Its fruits are red, turning almost black when fully ripe, and agreeable to the taste. It is the white mulberry (*M. alba*) that is grown chiefly for the sake of its leaves, upon which silkworms feed. Its fruits are pale green, turning pink when ripe, small and flavourless. It is of little interest to the home gardener and need not detain us here.

MULBERRIES IN BRITAIN

The black mulberry was brought to Britain by the Romans. Seeds of the fruit have been found at the site of Roman Silchester and, because the mulberry is a soft fruit that does not travel well, it seems that the trees must have been growing there.

They certainly grew in monastic gardens in medieval England. There was one, it seems, at Canterbury – a chronicler tells us that the knights who entered the cathedral to kill Thomas Becket in 1170 left their gowns outside under a mulberry tree. William Turner in 1551 waxed eloquent about the mulberry and at about the same time was planted the now-aged tree at Syon House, Brentford. Robert Hogg's *Herefordshire Pomona* confirms that by 1876 mulberries were fairly well represented in England.

MULBERRIES IN THE UNITED STATES OF AMERICA

The red mulberry (*Morus rubra*) is native to the eastern United States, and is common from New England to Iowa and south to the Gulf states, mainly as a valuable shade tree. Its large, sweet, almost black fruits were much liked by the Indians and its rather rough leaves, hairy on the undersides, encouraged early settlers to try, not very successfully, to establish a silk industry

Above: a mulberry tree. Opposite: black mulberries

in Jamestown, Virginia. (The white mulberry was later brought from China to the southern states, notably Georgia, in a further attempt to produce silk.) The Mexican mulberry, which reaches through Texas, New Mexico, and Arizona, is also an American native, but its berries are smaller and of inferior flavour.

CULTIVATION

Mulberry fruits turn almost black when ripe, as they begin to fall from mid-August onwards; from the big trees found in some old gardens picking up off the grass beneath, rather than from the tree, is about the only way to harvest the crop. To defeat blackbirds and thrushes you need to net the tree as the fruits begin to colour up until it becomes so big and the fruits so

'Pendula', the weeping white mulberry

numerous that you can afford to share them. They are borne on the current year's shoots, also on spurs off the older wood, and ripen over several weeks throughout August and September.

The mulberry likes a deep, well-drained, and fertile soil. It prefers a sheltered site, but is hardy in zones 5–8. It grows rather slowly to its full height of about 25 ft (7.5 m) and can be grown as a bush, pyramid, or half standard. It can also be trained on a wall or wire fence, but pruning needs to be kept to a minimum as the stem bleeds when cut. A mulberry may even, if it is started young, be successfully grown in a tub for a number of years.

Mulberries normally need little attention. If the tree is growing in a lawn, the grass must be kept clear of the stem for a radius of about 1 ft 6 in (45 cm). Water should be given freely in dry spells. If a young tree is being slow to produce full-size and healthy-looking foliage a general fertilizer should be applied in spring.

The minute, green flowers appear in spring, before or with the leaves. The mulberry is self-pollinating and will fruit if grown as a single plant. The fruits are borne on the current year's shoots and on spurs off the older wood, and ripen over several weeks throughout August and September. A useful quantity of fruit can be gathered from a fairly young tree.

Mulberries are usually propagated from cuttings or layers. When grown from seed, germination can be irregular and trees are slower to come into bearing.

The only troublesome disease that can affect mulberries in Britain is a canker that attacks young shoots, usually after cold damp weather. Affected shoots should be removed and burned.

Large Black is a grafted variety, presumably a selected clone, that makes an attractive, spreading tree. The fruits may be used for cooking or for dessert.

NECTARINES

The nectarine (*Prunus persica nectarina*) is a sport or mutation of the peach. It is really only a peach with a smooth skin and this is the chief difference between them, apart from the juicier taste and brighter colouring of the nectarine. The flavour is responsible for its name, from nectar, the drink of the gods.

NECTARINES IN BRITAIN

Nectarines were first listed separately from peaches by John Rea in 1676. Other 17th-century writers were already emphasizing that they needed to be grown against the hottest walls or under protection. By 1777 Richard Weston included 11 nectarines in his catalogue and by 1826 the Royal Horticultural Society listed 72 as growing in its gardens at Chiswick – although many must have been duplicated under synonyms.

In the 19th century Thomas Rivers worked on the breeding of new nectarines. He produced 'Pine Apple' and 'Lord Napier' in the 1860s, 'Humboldt' in the 1870s, and about fifteen other varieties not now being grown. 'Early Rivers' came in 1893 from his son Thomas Francis. In 1909 his grandson, Thomas Alfred, was listing 23 varieties, mostly introduced by his nursery. In the 1930s the Rivers catalogue and those of Bunyard and Laxton all listed 14 varieties. The flesh of some ('clingstones') clung to the stone and of others ('freestones') came away freely; some were more perfumed than others; and flesh colours varied between white, yellow, and reddish.

Recommended varieties
All the varieties named below bear rose-pink flowers and are self-fertile.

Lord Napier is the most widely grown variety and generally recommended as the hardiest for outdoor growing, although it can equally well be grown under glass. The flesh is white, melting, and very juicy and ripens in early August. The skin is yellow, flushed crimson, and exceedingly tempting. It was raised by Rivers in 1869, a seedling from a now-forgotten variety, 'Early Albert'.

Early Rivers is equally reliable for outdoors or for under glass, having white flesh, richly flavoured. The skin is light yellow with crimson colouring, ripening at

'Early Rivers' growing under glass

the end of July, about a fortnight ahead of 'Lord Napier'. It was raised by Thomas Francis Rivers, using 'Stanwick' as a parent, and introduced in 1893.

Elruge, white-fleshed, with excellent flavour, has greenish-white skin and a dark red flush. It has done well in damp conditions but is usually recommended for growing under glass. The fruits, which can be smaller than those of other varieties, are ready at the end of August. 'Elruge' is (almost) an anagram of Gurle, the name of its raiser, a nurseryman of Hoxton in the reign of Charles II.

Humboldt has large, tender, juicy, fruits with orange flesh and bright yellow skin with crimson flush and mottlings; it is very fertile and ready mid-August. It was a seedling grown by Rivers from 'Pine Apple' and introduced in 1872.

John Rivers is similar in colouring to 'Early Rivers', but it fruits earlier, ripening in mid-July. Named for Thomas Rivers's grandfather, it was introduced between 1910 and 1933.

Pine Apple has yellow flesh and orange skin with a red cheek; it ripens in early September and is probably rather tender for growing outdoors. Perhaps the

'Early Rivers'

'Humboldt' growing in a conservatory

richest-flavoured of the nectarines, it was raised by Thomas Rivers from 'Pitmaston Orange', which was a seedling of 'Elruge'.

Nectarina is a genetic dwarf nectarine grafted on St Julien A rootstock for a good root system. It reaches a height of about 4 ft 6 in (1.4 m) at maturity, is self-fertile, and bears full-size fruits that have yellow, very juicy flesh. These dwarf trees can be grown in tubs or large pots or trained against a low wall or fence.

NECTARINES IN THE UNITED STATES OF AMERICA

Nectarines have been widely grown in the United States in recent years, especially in California – so much so that they have become, for commercial growers, virtually a Pacific-coast fruit. The thin skin demands careful handling and transporting, however, so for the home gardener this is an ideal fruit to grow if conditions allow. The culture is the same as for peaches but nectarines can be more susceptible to brown rot disease in the hot and humid conditions of southern gardens. The mild winters and humid summers in the Gulf states and southern California are not suitable because a certain amount of winter chill is essential.

No satisfactory dwarfing rootstock is available but the new genetically controlled dwarf cultivars, which grow only to 4–6 ft (1.2–1.8 m) in height, can easily be grown in containers or small spaces and need very little pruning to produce good crops of full-size fruits. Numerous cultivars have been bred, sharing a common heritage from two Chinese genetic dwarf peaches named 'Swataw' and 'Flory'. All are yellow-fleshed with red skins. 'Nectarina', 'Garden Delight', 'Garden King', and 'Southern Belle' are low-chill cultivars needing 300–400 hours below 45° F (7° C), suitable for zones 5–10. 'Golden Prolific' has a high-chill requirement (900 hours) and is suitable for zones 5–8. 'Sunbonnet' is medium-chill, needing 500 hours, and is suitable for zones 5–9.

Recommended varieties

While nectarines are normally self-fertile, in warmer parts of the United States cross-pollination, where two or more are planted near to each other, can improve the set. From the cultivars now available in the United States, the following are recommended for home gardens. They are listed in approximate order of ripening.

Early varieties

Independence (zones 6–9) has brilliant red, oval fruit with freestone and firm yellow flesh, standing warm winters in the south and west. It is a productive variety with showy blossom.

Silver Lode (zones 6–9) is white-fleshed and freestone with red skin, sweet and firm, ripening over a long period. From California, it requires little winter chill.

Sunred (zones 8–10) came from Florida and is a very low-chill variety. Its small, red fruits have clingstone yellow flesh.

Mid-season varieties

Fantasia (zones 5–9), from California, is yellow-skinned with red blush and firm, yellow, freestone flesh. It is susceptible to disease but good for the south and west.

Flavortop (zones 6–9) has large, mostly red fruit and freestone yellow flesh. Best in the south and west.

Mericrest (zones 5–8) originated at the University of New Hampshire and has proved to be very winter hardy and disease resistant. It has red skin and freestone yellow flesh.

Panamint (zones 6–10), from California, is good for the south and west. Vigorous and productive, it needs little winter chill. Red-skinned fruits have freestone yellow flesh.

Late-season varieties

Redgold (zones 5–8) is good for north and south. The skin is glossy red, the freestone flesh firm and yellow, red around the stone. Watch for mildew.

Gold Mine (zones 5–9) is a favourite old variety, its large fruits having white skin blushed red, with juicy, white, freestone flesh. It originated in New Zealand.

Fairlane (zones 5–9) is a very late-ripening Californian variety with red-skinned fruit and yellow, clingstone flesh. Good for the west, it makes a vigorous tree that bears regularly.

CULTIVATION

Where a district is too unkind even for a sunny wall to protect a nectarine, it must be grown in a conservatory. A compromise is to grow a nectarine as a bush in a large pot, so that it may be carried outdoors after picking the fruit and taken in before frosts. A certain amount of chilling ripens the wood and improves the fruiting quality. For growing in pots it is best to start with a maiden tree (one-year-old, unpruned), whose roots will be easier to trim and pot than older trees. Replace the top inch or so of the compost each winter. Feed monthly from April to August with a liquid general fertilizer.

The nectarine is self-fertile. It produces its fruit on the previous year's shoots and on spurs off older wood. No pruning should be done when the tree is dormant because this may lead to the entry of fungal disease. Pruning is best done in May or after picking the fruit. Peach leaf curl is the chief problem and treatment should be given as recommended for peaches. Nectarines grow and are treated exactly like peaches, but they need even more water at the roots to help swell the fruit. They are grafted on the semi-dwarfing rootstock St Julien A – the newer, dwarfing stock Pixy is not compatible. They can be bought as maidens, bushes, or fan-trained trees, the last being the most popular for planting against a sheltered south-facing wall, allowing a wall space about 15 ft (4.5 m) wide and at least 5 ft (1.5 m) high.

PEACHES

The blossom of 'Peregrine'

Peaches (*Prunus persica*) have always grown wild in northern parts of China and Korea, having been recorded there almost 4,000 years ago. The Greeks and Romans found peaches growing in Persia and, thinking they originated there, gave them the name 'persica'. Fruits or seeds probably reached Asia Minor along the old silk route from China and were planted around the eastern Mediterranean.

PEACHES IN BRITAIN

Edward I planted two peach trees in the garden of the Tower of London in 1275 and Chaucer, writing in 1372, referred to the many 'homely' trees of peaches, quinces, and apples. Later, in the 16th century, William Turner included peaches in his *Newe Herball* and John Gerard described four types of peach in his *Herball*. John Parkinson in 1629 knew of 21 peaches, some of which had been introduced to Britain by John Tradescant.

By 1826 the Royal Horticultural Society was listing 224 peaches in its collection at Chiswick, many of which must have been under synonyms, as the number was reduced by 1831 to 183, of which 60 were then being grown in English gardens or nurseries. 'Royal George', 'Bellegarde' ('Galande' in France), and 'Barrington' were some of the varieties included that are still well known today .

Thomas Francis Rivers, who continued his father's work in the family nursery, found the demand for peaches to be so good in his time that he worked hard at raising new varieties — 'Duke of York', 'Early Rivers', and 'Peregrine' came from his firm and are still with us today. Others popular in the 1930s and still grown — 'Hale's Early', 'Amsden June', 'Redhaven', and 'Rochester' — came from the United States.

Opposite: the fruits of a wall-trained 'Peregrine'

Recommended varieties

Duke of York, ripening in mid-July, is about the earliest peach. The fruits are large, with a brilliant crimson skin; the flesh is tender and pale yellow, with a clinging stone. 'Duke of York' crops well under glass. If planted outside it needs a particularly favourable and sunny wall. It was bred in 1902 from the nectarine 'Early Rivers' crossed with 'Alexander' peach.

Peregrine ripens early in August with firm, greeny-white freestone flesh of good flavour, the prolific fruits being large, round, and crimson. It is generally agreed to be first choice as a hardy cultivar for planting outside on a wall or it can be grown as a bush in a favourable site in the open. It was raised in 1906, a seedling from the nectarine 'Spenser'.

Rochester, ripening in mid-August, has yellow freestone flesh, firm and well flavoured; the fruit is yellow with a crimson flush. As this cultivar flowers a little later it often misses late spring frosts and so can crop heavily in a rather less favourable site. In bush form it will be likely to give much better results than the old favourite 'Peregrine'. It was raised on a farm near Rochester, New York, in 1900.

I rate these the top three. I recommend also six others. There are no cross-pollination problems with peaches – all are self-fertile and can be planted alone. If cold weather at flowering time prevents bees from flying and doing the pollinating, it is worth trying hand-pollination with a soft brush or rabbit's tail.

Amsden June, ready in mid-July, has white flesh, juicy and sweet, the stone clinging until ripe. The skin is greeny-white with a red flush. It is only a moderate cropper, best as an early cultivar grown under glass. It was raised at Carthage, Missouri, in about 1865.

Hale's Early ripens in late July and has white freestone flesh, the fruits being medium-size and yellow with red mottling; a heavy cropper, often needing thinning, it freezes well. It was raised at Randolph, Ohio, and introduced in about 1860.

Redhaven, ripening in mid-August, has yellow flesh, red near the stone, and medium-size fruits, deep red over yellow. It crops well under glass or in the open. It was raised at the Agricultural Experiment Station, Southaven, Michigan, from 'Halehaven' × 'Kalhaven' and introduced in 1940.

Royal George ripens from late August to early September and has large fruits, pale yellow with a red flush, and white flesh, rich and highly flavoured. It is best grown under glass or on a very warm wall. It is a very old variety dating from the reign of George I.

Bellegarde, a late ripener in mid-September, has white flesh of rich flavour. The fruits are large and golden, almost covered with dark crimson. It is an old French variety of uncertain parentage, known in Britain since 1732, and best grown under glass or on a warm wall.

Garden Lady is an exciting new peach tree that has recently been introduced from New Zealand. It is a genetic dwarf; that is to say its genes ensure its dwarf habit so that, in order to keep its branches off the ground, it has to be grafted onto a short stem, usually St Julien A. It produces full-size fruits with a bright red flush on a yellow skin, sweet and juicy. It is ideal for planting in a tub, in a confined space near the house, or in a narrow border.

PEACHES IN THE UNITED STATES OF AMERICA

Early settlers arriving in America had probably never seen peaches grown in the open until they found the Indians growing them. They were soon planting their own orchards, mostly for the production of peach brandy, as no doubt those wild fruits were a bit sour. An orchard of 63,000 seedling trees, owned by a Mr Bayley in Accomac County, Virginia, and planted in 1814, yielded nearly 10,000 gallons of brandy only five years later. Peaches were also dried for winter eating.

In no other part of the world did the peach grow and fruit as well as in the more favoured parts of North America. The first peaches to have been named in the United States may have been 'Heath Cling' and 'Heath Free', grown on the farm of the Revolutionary general William Heath at Roxbury, Massachusetts. By the middle of the 19th century American peaches were being introduced and were proving successful in Britain. Today, American breeders, mainly in California, produce valuable new cultivars that are grown in all other peach-growing areas of the world, notably the extensive new Italian orchards.

The new genetic dwarf peaches are of great interest to home gardeners in the United States. Their small size enables them to be grown in confined spaces or in containers that can be moved around.

Recommended varieties

From the many cultivars available, this selection is recommended for the home garden. The peaches are listed in approximate order of ripening.

Early varieties

Fairhaven (zones 5–9) originated in Michigan and is hardy, with showy blossom. It has a large yellow fruit with a red cheek and freestone yellow flesh, red next to the stone.

Reliance (zones 5–9), from New Hampshire, is also very winter hardy and also has showy blossom. The red and yellow skin is over firm, yellow, freestone flesh.

Redhaven (zones 5–9), from Michigan, is a vigorous tree, productive of very fine peaches, deep red over yellow. It may need thinning. The yellow freestone flesh does not brown. 'Early Redhaven' is identical, but ripens a fortnight earlier. 'Compact Redhaven' is a dwarf-growing form, good in the north.

Mid-season varieties

Veteran (zones 6–8), raised in Ontario, is a favourite in Washington and Oregon. It is vigorous, reliable, and productive. The large fruits are yellow splashed with red and have yellow, freestone flesh.

Loring (zones 6–8), a reliable setter, came from Missouri. The medium-size, high-quality fruits are blushed red over yellow, with freestone yellow flesh.

Late season varieties

Cresthaven (zones 6–8) is a hardy variety that originated in Michigan. The red-over-gold fruit has non-browning flesh, freestone and yellow.

Madison (zones 5–8) came from Virginia. Its blossom has excellent resistance to frost. The fruits have bright red over orange skin with freestone orange-yellow flesh.

Belle of Georgia (zones 6–8), which originated in Georgia, is an outstanding white-fleshed peach of high quality with red-over-whitish skin. It is vigorous and winter hardy, but susceptible to brown rot.

Elberta (zones 5–9), another old favourite from Georgia, is resistant to brown rot and has large, freestone, red-over-gold fruit. The consistently productive 'Early Elberta' (Gleason strain), which is from Utah, ripens a week or so earlier and is of better flavour.

Redskin (zones 5–8) is a non-browning yellow freestone from Maryland. It has showy flowers over a long period and bears high-quality fruits that colour well, even in shade.

Rio-Oso-Gem (zones 6–9), from California, makes a small but productive tree with large, showy blossom, later than most other peaches. Fruit is of fine texture, the flesh being yellow freestone, non-browning.

There are numerous genetic dwarf peaches. The original, **Bonanza** (zones 6–9), which originated in California, is now well-tried. It is a yellow-fleshed freestone and has a moderate chill requirement (about 500 hours). Others include 'Empress', 'Garden Gold', 'Honey Babe', 'Southern Flame', 'Southern Rose', 'Southern Sweet', and 'Sunburst'.

CULTIVATION

The soil that suits peaches best is a deep, well-drained, medium loam. They do not thrive on a light sandy soil unless moisture retention has been greatly improved by the incorporation of organic matter. A shallow soil over chalk will be too dry and limey. If it is to be grown as a bush in the open, a sheltered position in full sun will give the peach the best chance.

St Julien A is the favourite rootstock for peaches these days; more vigorous stocks like Brompton, Myrobalan B, Mussel, and Mariana are no longer used and unfortunately the dwarfing Pixy has been found to be unsuitable; the bud-take is poor and the fruits on any resulting trees are small and dry. A peach can of course be grown from the seed inside the stone but it will take a long time to start fruiting and there is no guarantee that it will be worth eating when it does.

A point worth remembering in the cultivation of peaches is that the tree's roots need frequent watering while the fruits are swelling; they are largely composed of water and have to hold a stone inside them, so very small fruits are useless. The wall behind a trained peach tree inevitably soaks up a lot of the available moisture and its foundations take more again, so a tree growing against a wall may need up to twice as much water as one growing in the open. A mulch over the roots is a great help in preventing moisture from evaporating away in the summer.

Because peaches may flower while late spring frosts still threaten, it is important to protect the trees on cold nights when the flowers begin to open. It is easy enough to drop a fine mesh net, or a sheet of hessian or polythene, over a trained tree from the top of its wall. Remember, though, that this must not keep off the bees who will pollinate the flowers for you; it can be held off the tree with bamboo canes placed at an angle to the wall. Should the weather be too cold for the bees to be flying when the blossom is ready, you can pollinate by hand using a soft brush or rabbit's tail. The blossom of a peach tree is a springtime bonus in the garden.

To ensure good-sized peaches, the fruitlets should be thinned in June when about the size of hazel nuts, so that each remaining one has about a fist's width of space in which to swell. There is a natural thinning, like the June drop of apples, but this may not be enough so it is as well to check the trees a few weeks later in case more thinning is needed. At the same time, any leaves that fall across a peach should be removed to allow the sun to shine directly upon the fruit.

The initial formative pruning of peach trees is the same as for other fruits, except that it is never done in winter because of the risk of disease entering. Pruning the cropping tree should always be aimed toward ensuring an adequate supply of new wood to carry next year's fruit and toward restricting extension growth from old wood. In May, shoots growing inwards against a wall or fence and at right-angles outwards are removed, leaving only one or two leaves if they have a thick flower bud at the base. The previous year's laterals are pinched back to leave three side shoots only – the bottom one to form a replacement shoot, the middle one in reserve, and the top one to extend the fruit-carrying shoot. When the two basal shoots are about 15–18 in (40–45 cm) long

and the extension lateral has six leaves, the growing points are pinched out.

When the leaves develop red blisters and then curl up somewhat grotesquely, this denotes the presence of the unsightly disease called peach leaf curl, the chief problem likely to be met in peach growing. It usually arrives as the young leaves open in spring, the blisters being yellow at first, then red, and finally covering the leaf in a fine white bloom. Although peach leaf curl does not kill the tree, it slows growth and leads to dieback if unchecked. The recommended control has always been to spray with a copper fungicide on the dormant wood in January or February, repeating the dose two weeks later. This is not as effective as one might wish – it is better to prevent rain falling on the branches between December and mid-May.

It is in this period that the airborne spores that produce the fungus get washed by rain on to the leaf buds. So the best preventive treatment is to cover the peach tree with polythene to ward off rain in these months. Against a wall, it is not too difficult to erect a frame that can support first a frost-protection and later the polythene rain cover and also keep away marauding birds. Bush peaches in the open also need protection, although admittedly this is a little more difficult to provide. Some sort of polythene tent or umbrella might seem to be a solution.

Dwarf peach trees in the Halifax Courtyard Garden at the 1986 Chelsea Flower Show

PEARS

The common pear (*Pyrus communis*) probably originated in western Asia. Like the apple, it was used as food by Stone Age men in neighbouring parts of Europe. The ancient Greeks knew it and the Romans spread it throughout temperate Europe. Murals in the ruins of Pompeii depict pears among the fruits grown there before the eruption of Vesuvius in AD 79.

PEARS IN BRITAIN

It was the Romans who introduced pears to Britain and the monasteries that preserved the art of pear growing after they left. British monks, with their connections with continental Europe, soon brought in new varieties of pear from France, and French varieties remained popular for centuries afterward. In the 13th century Henry III and his queen, Eleanor of Provence, and Edward I and his queen, Eleanor of Castile, planted pears known to have been mostly imported from France, although their names are now forgotten. In 1553 Henry VIII's fruiterer, Richard Harris, brought pears from France and Belgium for planting in the king's orchards.

The 'Warden' cooking pear was introduced before the end of the 12th century by the Cistercian monks of Warden Abbey in Bedfordshire. 'Hot-baked Wardens'

A pear tunnel at Langford House, Bristol University

were sold on the London streets as late as 1703. The 'Black Worcester' pear, which appears in the coat of arms of the city, is another old culinary variety – it was grown in Worcestershire before 1575. Other old varieties are still being grown today. 'Jargonelle' dates from before 1600 and 'Catillac' from before 1645. 'Glou Morceau' was raised in 1759, 'Williams' Bon Chrétien' *c*. 1770, and 'Louise Bonne of Jersey'*c*. 1780.

The controlled breeding of pears was left mainly to the famous fruit nurseries of Rivers and Laxton in the late 19th and early 20th centuries. Rivers produced 'Fertility' in about 1875 from seed of 'Beurré Goubalt' and it was planted quite freely in gardens.

Laxton's Nurseries did a lot of work on pears in the years up to World War II, mostly using as either seed or pollen parents the varieties 'Marie Louise', 'Williams' Bon Chrétien', 'Doyenné du Comice', 'Beurré Superfin', 'Fertility', and 'Durondeau'. Of the resulting new pears, 'Laxton's Superb' showed the most promise – it was an excellent, very juicy, early pear that proved also to be a good pollinator for

'Doyenné du Comice'. Unfortunately, though, it proved to be vulnerable to fireblight disease and it was eventually banned by the Ministry of Agriculture in the 1960s. There was a real fear that, if allowed to get out of hand, fireblight could spread from the fruit orchards to the quickthorn hedges of the countryside.

Recommended varieties

Today there is a collection of nearly 500 different pear trees in the National Fruit Trials at the Ministry of Agriculture's Brogdale Farm near Faversham, Kent. But the Royal Horticultural Society, in the *Fruit Garden Displayed* (1986), recommends only 24 pear varieties for garden planting. I find from a study of nursery catalogues that about seventeen varieties are fairly readily obtainable. These are described here in the approximate order in which they were raised. To decide on suitable pollinators, reference should be made to the Flowering Table on page 151; the pollinating group to which each pear belongs is specified in the text.

Williams' Bon Chrétien (Group 3), usually shortened to 'Williams'', must be the most famous pear of all. It was raised in England in about 1770, having been discovered, and planted in his garden, by a Mr Wheeler, the schoolmaster at Aldermaston, Berkshire. The garden was taken over by the next schoolmaster, Mr Stair, who named it 'Stair's Pear' and who allowed Richard Williams, a nurseryman of Turnham Green, Middlesex, to distribute it. Williams gave the variety his own name, with 'Bon Chrétien' added, possibly because he believed the seed parent to have been 'Bon Chrétien d'Hiver', an old and respected variety. The Rivers catalogue of 1881 still listed it as 'Bon Chrétien Williams'; only later was the name turned around. 'Williams'' was very favourably received when first exhibited in 1816 and Robert Hogg thought it to be one of the finest pears in 1862, but it received an Award of Merit only in 1970. It has been exported widely and is now one of the very few pears of British origin to be planted worldwide. Wherever grown it keeps its sweet, musky flavour, melting tenderness, and great juiciness. In Britain it is ready to eat in September. It spurs freely to make cordons but has to be watched for scab.

Glou Morceau (Group 4) is a late-flowering pear that ripens slowly for eating in December and January. The name is derived from the Flemish 'golou' meaning delicious and from 'morceau', a morsel. Its parentage is unknown, but it was raised by the Abbé Hardenpont of Mons in Belgium in 1759. The Abbé was a pioneer of pear hybridizing and Edward Bunyard thought it a

Pear shapes – 1 'Merton Pride'; 2 'Bristol Cross'; 3 'Williams' Bon Chrétien'; 4 'Improved Fertility'; 5 'Pitmaston Duchess'; 6 'Onward'; 7 'Conference'; 8 'Beth'

'Williams' Bon Chrétien'

pity that his name was not commemorated in this cultivar, one of our best late pears. Rich and sugary-flavoured, 'Glou Morceau' seems to do best in a sheltered place or on a sunny wall and has moderate, rather spreading growth.

Louise Bonne of Jersey (Group 2), another pear of unknown parentage, was raised in about 1780 in Avranches, France. It has the enviable reputation of being a regular and profuse bearer and a well-behaved cultivar in most situations. The red-flushed, distinctively flavoured fruits, covered in prominent dots, are ready in late October. It flowers earlier than most, so likes a frost-protected position. It has a shapely, fairly upright habit that is not difficult to control.

Durondeau (Group 3) was raised by the grower after whom it is named in Tongre, Belgium, in 1811. It is a

remarkably fertile and regular cropper, compact in habit. The large fruits are a rich russet brown with crimson flush. The flesh is melting and well flavoured when ripe in late October or November, and keeps well in store. The leaves turn an attractive red in autumn.

Winter Nelis (Group 4), another late-flowering cultivar of unknown parentage, was raised at Malines, Belgium, in 1815. It has small, russetted fruits with a rich, buttery, almost wine-like flavour that keep well in store and are best eaten in December and January. 'Winter Nelis' probably reaches its best when grown on a warm wall, as it has a somewhat thin, weeping habit.

Beurré Hardy (Group 3) is a very hardy pear, but that is not the reason for its name; raised in about 1820 at Boulogne, it was named after the Director of the Luxembourg Gardens, whose surname was Hardy. It makes vigorous, somewhat upright growth and can be slow to come into full bearing. It is disease-resistant

with a russet-red skin, rosewater scent, and tender flesh for eating in October.

Josephine de Malines (Group 3) was raised from unknown parentage in 1830 at Malines, Belgium. The raiser, Major Esperen, a veteran of Napoleon's army, named it after his wife. Its blossom is fairly frost-resistant and the fruits have the happy habit of ripening reliably over a longer period than most, through December into January. Its pinkish flesh is both rich to taste and rose-perfumed, mellow, and juicy. It makes a small tree with rather weeping habit, tending to tip-bearing and responding best to light pruning and to festooning, rather than normal harder pruning.

Doyenné du Comice (Group 4) was raised by the Horticultural Society of the French department of Maine-et-Loire at Angers, where the tree first fruited in 1849. It was introduced to England in 1858 by Sir Thomas Dyke-Acland for his garden at Killerton,

Above: 'Beurré Hardy'. Opposite: 'Doyenné du Comice'

Devon. It is generally agreed to be the finest-flavoured pear grown today but, like a 'Cox's Orange Pippin' apple, it can be difficult to manage. It is easily bruised and so should be harvested unripe and handled as little as possible before being stored in a cool place until ready to eat, usually late in October and through November. This is when the colour has changed from green to yellow under its coating of russet and the perfect combination of aroma, flavour, and texture is reached, with the buttery flesh ready to melt in the mouth.

Pitmaston Duchess (Group 4) was raised in 1841 by John Williams of Pitmaston, Worcestershire, its parentage being 'Duchesse d'Angoulême' × 'Glou Morceau'. Being a late-flowerer it often misses spring frosts but it is a triploid and therefore no use as a pollinator. It ripens in late October and into November with a fine golden-yellow skin and slight russetting

Above: a fan-trained 'Doyenné du Comice' tree in blossom. Left: a 'Doyenné du Comice' tree. Opposite: 'Conference'

with yellow flesh. 'Pitmaston Duchess' is also popular with exhibitors who like a big fruit and with cooks, who describe it as a dual-purpose pear. The Royal Horticultural Society gave it a First Class Certificate in 1874 but its vigorous growth and a proneness to scab make it less suitable for the small garden.

Conference (Group 3) is easily the most widely planted pear in Britain today. It was raised by Thomas Francis Rivers, who chaired the 1888 International Fruit Conference at which it was first exhibited and after which it was named. Rivers had taken seed from an open-pollinated tree of 'Léon Leclerc de Laval', a cooking variety raised in Belgium in 1825. A trial planting of 25 'Conference' trees was made in 1895 and the first commercial orchard established soon afterward at Allington, near Maidstone, Kent. The variety quickly became popular with other growers on account of its pleasant flavour, ease of pollination, heavy cropping, and good storage capability. Being self-fertile, a tree of 'Conference' can set fruits with its own pollen, but typical pears are then long and thin, although seedless. The pears are ready for eating in October and November.

Packham's Triumph (Group 2) is grown by a number of nurseries, but not thought highly of by the Royal Horticultural Society. It is an Australian pear raised in New South Wales in about 1896 and said to be a seedling from 'Uvedale's St Germain' × 'Williams' Bon Chrétien'. It has bright yellow fruits with much russetting, the white flesh being juicy and having a

A fan-trained 'Conference' pear tree growing in the Royal Horticultural Society Garden at Wisley

musky flavour. It flowers early, and the fruit is ready for eating in November. It makes upright and compact growth.

Gorham (Group 4) was raised in the United States and introduced to Britain in 1923. It spurs freely and makes compact growth but crops only moderately, with juicy, musky-flavoured, small-to-medium fruits coming between 'Williams' Bon Chrétien' and 'Conference' in late September.

Improved Fertility (Group 4) is an improved clone of 'Fertility', a pear of Rivers' raising. It was noticed growing at Seabrooks' Nurseries at Boreham, Essex, in 1934. It has rather small fruits, heavily russetted and produced in abundance, bigger when carefully thinned. They are sweet and juicy when ripe in late September or October and can be cooked or bottled. It is self-fertile, flowering late and is a disease-resistant cultivar with colourful autumn foliage. Although not in the first class and a suspect for canker, it is very fertile and hardy enough for unfavourable sites.

Beth (Group 4) was raised at East Malling in 1938 by H. M. Tydeman, but not introduced until 1974. Its parentage is 'Beurré Superfin' × 'Williams' Bon Chrétien' (the same as the ill-fated 'Laxton's Superb'). It has not been taken up by commercial growers, possibly because of their investment in 'Williams' Bon Chrétien' as the most popular early pear, but it is a good cultivar for gardens. The fruits are ready in September and medium in size, with creamy white flesh, melting and juicy, the flavour being rich and sweet. The skin colour is pale yellow, sometimes tinged pink, with a golden russet. 'Beth' spurs freely and begins to bear soon after planting.

Onward (Group 4) is a variety raised at the National Fruit Trials in 1947; it has the promising parentage of 'Laxton's Superb' × 'Doyenné du Comice' and it received the Award of Merit in 1967. It makes a fairly vigorous tree with plenty of fruit spurs. The medium-sized fruits are greeny-yellow flushed with red and have creamy flesh of excellent flavour, juicy and melting, ready late September and into October.

Merton Pride (Group3) was raised in 1941 at the John Innes Horticultural Institution by Morley Crane, who was largely responsible for the introduction of all the cultivars that bear the 'Merton' prefix. It was at first called 'Merton Favourite', but renamed in 1957 on introduction. It was given the Award of Merit in 1973 and the First Class Certificate in 1983. Its parentage was 'Glou Morceau' × 'Double Williams'' (an American sport of 'Williams' Bon Chrétien') and its large pears are golden-yellow, almost covered in russet; they have exceptional flavour, are very juicy and sweet and melting in the mouth, ripening from the middle to late September. 'Merton Pride' has certain disadvantages for the small garden. It is a triploid variety and unsuitable as a pollinator; it is partially biennial – that is, it bears only a light crop in alternate years; and it suffers greatly from bird damage, from bullfinches in particular. It has never been taken up commercially, but, in spite of its disadvantages, it is valued highly by pear enthusiasts for its superb flavour.

Concorde (Group 4) is a very new pear, released in 1988, raised at East Malling Research Station by Dr Frank Alston from 'Doyenné du Comice' × 'Conference'. It is similar in appearance to 'Conference', but is tastier. It has a peak flowering time four or five days later than 'Conference', which makes it an ideal cross-pollinator with 'Doyenné du Comice'. A heavy cropper, it is picked later than 'Conference' and is best eaten in late October and November.

PEARS IN THE UNITED STATES OF AMERICA

Pears, especially on dwarf rootstocks, are ideal home-garden fruit trees – they have lovely blossom, bear early in life, need little pruning, and take easily to training if desired. In some areas they are prone to fireblight, at its worst in spring, so a watch must be kept; there are resistant varieties to choose from. It is of course important to plant cross-pollinating varieties.

'Seckel'

Some of the best for home gardens are described below, in approximate order of ripening.

Recommended varieties
Moonglow (zones 5–9) comes from Maryland and bears, early in the season, large, attractive pears that are soft, juicy, and mild-flavoured. The tree spurs heavily, fruits when young, and resists fireblight.

Orient (zones 5–10) originated in California. It is resistant to fireblight and its mild-flavoured fruit, round in shape and with firm flesh, preserves well.

Bartlett (zones 5–8) is the variety known as 'Williams' Bon Chrétien' in Britain. It was brought to America in 1797 by James Carter of Boston and planted in a garden at Roxbury, Massachusetts. The garden passed in 1817 to Enoch Bartlett, who gave the tree his own name, being unaware of its origins. It is best left to commercial growers in fireblight areas, but elsewhere is good wherever there is adequate winter chill. Its fruit is yellow and thin-skinned, with sweet, juicy flesh, and is much used for canning. 'Red Bartlett', a smaller tree from Australia, has pears heavily blushed with red. 'Winter Bartlett' matures later.

Magness (zones 5–8), from Maryland, bears light crops of medium-sized oval fruits, of excellent quality, slightly russetted and highly perfumed. The tree is vigorous and highly resistant to fireblight; it is not a pollinator for other pears.

Maxine (zones 5–10) originated in Ohio and has strong resistance to fireblight. It bears large, attractive pears, firm and juicy with sweet white flesh. Sometimes sold under the name 'Starking Delicious', it could be a better choice than a 'Bartlett' for home gardens.

Anjou ('Beurré d'Anjou') originated in France near the Loire and is not for areas with hot summers or where fireblight is a problem. It keeps well and bears large, green pears with firm flesh of mild flavour which turn yellow when ripe.

Comice (zones 5–10) is the pear known in Britain as 'Doyenné du Comice'. It has adapted well to the western coastal states and bears large yellow-green fruits, aromatic and juicy, very fine for dessert. It may need cool storage to ripen properly.

Gorham (zones 5–9) was raised in 1910 at the New York State Experimental Station, from 'Williams' Bon Chrétien' × 'Josephine de Malines'. It is a vigorous, fertile tree with excellent fruit resembling 'Bartlett' but ripening later and keeping longer.

Kieffer (zones 5–10) originated in Pennsylvania. The large yellow fruits can be gritty but keep well and are useful for preserving. 'Kieffer' is very resistant to fireblight, needs little winter chill, and stands both heat and cold.

Seckel (zones 5–9) was found in a wood near Philadelphia, in the early years of the 19th century, by a trapper known as Dutch Jacob. It is a highly productive and fireblight-resistant tree, although somewhat biennial. It bears small, yellow-brown fruits with a fine aroma and good honeyed flavour.

Bosc (zones 5–9) – sometimes known as 'Beurré Bosc' or 'Golden Russet' – was bred by Van Mons in Belgium and introduced in the 1840s. It has large, high-quality pears useful for showing, with russet skin, tender, juicy flesh, and a pleasing aroma. It makes a vigorous tree but is susceptible to fireblight.

ASIAN PEARS

Most Asian, or apple, pears originate in Japan, although some come from China. They are not crosses between apples and pears, but a distinctly different fruit with a unique flavour – the flesh is crisp, juicy and quite sweet, a little gritty compared with European pears. The fruits are now available from the shops, and the trees from a few nurseries, on both sides of the Atlantic. In Britain fifteen cultivars are being grown at the National Fruit Trials in Kent.

The pearly-pink blossom is very decorative in spring and is said to be resistant to frosts. Asian pears are not self-fertile, so need pollinating by any other pears in flower at the same time. They keep a lot longer in store than most pears and are eaten firm, more like big russet apples. In Britain fruits ripen in late September or early October; they should be picked when ripe, like apples, not early for indoor ripening, like European pears.

Asian pears should thrive in Britain wherever pears normally succeed and may in fact prove to be hardier. In the United States they grow well on the west coast and in the south and east, where fireblight can be avoided, generally in zones 5–9. They are being grown on Quince A rootstocks in Britain but in America Asian stocks may be used where these are found to be preferable. They are pruned and trained like apple and pear trees and make good espaliers.

Chojuro is flat and russet-skinned with strong flavour and firm flesh, bearing regularly and storing well.

Hosui has golden-brown skin over a large apple-shaped fruit with fine-textured and juicy, sweet flesh; it stores well.

Kikusui is flat and yellow-skinned, very juicy and mild-flavoured, best picked as it begins to turn yellow.

Kumoi has crisp, juicy, and very sweet, apple-like fruits that keep well; the tree is vigorous and not sensitive to frost.

Nijisseiki ('Twentieth Century' in California) has a flat, greenish fruit. It tends to be biennial, but this can be controlled by thinning in the heavy-cropping 'on' year.

Shinseiki is probably the earliest Asian pear to ripen. It bears flat pears, best picked as they turn yellow.

Shinko is perhaps the heaviest-bearing Asian. Its golden-russet fruits have good texture and rich flavour and keep well.

Ya Li, which originated in China, bears pear-shaped, fine-textured fruit. It is partially self-fertile but is better with a pollinator, which must of course match its early flowering. It has a low chill requirement.

Other Asian pears undergoing trials are 'Choju', 'Hakko', 'Kosui', 'Niitaka', 'Shinsui', 'Tama', and 'Yakumo'.

CULTIVATION

Pear trees are grown just like apples, but they demand a little more effort to bring them to perfection. The main rules for successful pear growing are:

Start with healthy trees from a reliable source and choose the right cultivars to ensure cross-pollination.

Give them a well-drained, rich, deep soil that does not dry out too quickly in summer.

Give them a position sheltered from cold winds and protected from frost at blossom time, where they will get plenty of sun in summer.

Prune them carefully, as recommended for apples.

Protect the fruit buds from marauding birds, particularly bullfinches, in late winter.

ROOTSTOCKS

In the mid-16th century pears, although mostly grafted on seedlings grown from pear pips, were sometimes grafted on hawthorn seedlings, which belong to the same botanical family. These grew long thong-like tap roots with poor fibrous systems that had the effect of making the scions grafted on them grow very vigorously and take their time about coming into bearing, from which arises the old adage 'plant pears for your heirs'. Later, quince was considered, particularly by the French, as a suitable alternative rootstock but it was not widely accepted, partly because some varieties were incompatible with it and had to be double-grafted.

In our time, though, quince is used almost exclusively. Quince A is the rootstock most used for trees destined for garden planting while Quince C is used mainly for trees ordered for commercial orchards. The currently popular clone of 'Conference', however, does not take well from budding on either Quince stock and is normally grafted instead. Quince A is said to be more frost-resistant than C and to crop sooner. Quince C induces dwarfer trees, although it is not quite so definite in its influence over its scions as is M.27 for apples (see page 91); it needs good soil conditions for success.

Whichever rootstock your pear trees are grafted on it is important to plant with the union of stock and scion well above ground level. Where earth is allowed to cover the graft scion rooting takes place and leads to over-vigorous, rather upright growth with poor fruiting, both in number and size.

PICKING AND STORING

Pears need more careful picking than apples because they bruise easily and then quickly start to rot. It is important to pick with the stalk intact – a longish thumbnail helps if the fruit hangs on tightly. A pressure test on the pear is not a reliable guide to a picking date. Pick pears before they ripen fully, because they do not taste their best straight off the tree; if they are harvested too early, however, they sometimes shrivel. My 'Conference' tree is best picked in late September or early October, while the fruit is still green; if left much longer on the tree the pears start to turn yellow and then do not keep well in store.

I stand my pears on newspaper, with rolls of paper between the rows, in shallow trays stacked together in a fruit rack. The rack needs to be in a cool place, standing out of the sun and in the darkest corner, or in a cellar if available. (Remember to put down traps to catch mice and voles if you store in an outbuilding.) The pears are not wrapped individually, so that frequent inspections quickly reveal any that need removing; once pears turn yellow or a light brown they are ripening fast and need eating. I bring mine indoors a few at a time to ripen fully in the warmth – a softening on the top of the pear beside the stalk tells me when it is nearly ready. To protect fruit in store if severe frosts are likely, I wrap the rack in polythene – pears freeze at $28°F (-2°C)$.

PLUMS, GAGES, AND DAMSONS

The plum we know today in our gardens is *Prunus domestica*. Its parents are *P. spinosa*, the blackthorn or sloe, and *P. cerasifera*, the cherry plum. These two species, which grow together in Asia Minor, have interbred over thousands of years to give us the range of fruits we call plums. From another species, *P. insititia*, we get our modern gages, *P. i. italica*. *P. insititia* grows in the wild in Europe; it is known as the bullace in Britain and as the mirabelle in France. It was probably from *P. insititia* also that the damsons evolved in the Middle East and they have their own status, *P. damascena*, a name taken from the city of Damascus, around which the fruit has been grown for over 2,000 years. Damsons have a dry, sweet-yet-bitter taste not found in plums and gages; they are closer to the bullaces. The fruits of *P. insititia*, although small, are sweet and nicely scented and it is these two qualities that distinguish gages from plums. The bullace and the mirabelle are hardly worth giving garden room to and, in any case, they rarely appear in fruit catalogues these days.

PLUMS AND GAGES IN BRITAIN

The gage came to Britain under the name 'verdoch', an anglicization of the Italian *verdocchia*, the name under which it arrived in France during the reign of Francis I (1515–47). The king named the gage, after his queen, 'Reine Claude'. Two hundred years later, in about 1720–24, Sir William Gage of Hengrave Hall, near Bury St Edmunds, received a tree of 'Reine Claude' from France. It was sent to him, it seems, by a Jesuit priest living near Paris, John Gage, probably a cousin or brother, and a native of Suffolk. The tree's label was lost, so Sir William's gardener named it 'Green Gage' after his employer. The name stuck, and was used by nurserymen from then onward.

As 'Reine Claude', or '(Old) Green Gage', reproduces itself true to name when grown from root suckers the variety has remained fairly constant, although trees that are virtually the same have appeared with different names periodically, among them 'Cambridge Gage' and 'Early Transparent Gage'.

Plums were certainly eaten in Britain in Roman times, because plum stones have been found in Roman remains around London, but the trees may not have been grown in Britain, as they certainly were in Rome. British references from the 15th century indicate that plums were mostly preserved or dried before eating, no doubt because the varieties then available were rather sour, like those still being picked in the wild. With little knowledge of grafting or hybridizing, progress towards more acceptable dessert varieties was extremely slow. However, the improved varieties of tree fruits from Europe whose planting Henry VIII encouraged included plums, probably better sorts than are indicated by the plum stones raised from the wreck of his warship *Mary Rose* (see page 11). Soon after Henry's death, William Turner mentioned 'divers kyndes of plumbes' growing in England and in 1597, John Gerard claimed to have at least sixty varieties of plum and damson in his garden. The Tradescants are known to have brought in more varieties early in the 17th century.

Thomas Rivers raised or introduced over a dozen good plums. The first was 'Rivers Early Prolific', from seed of 'Précoce de Tours', which he introduced in about 1834; within a short time his nursery was selling up to 20,000 trees annually. There followed 'Czar' in 1874, the result of crossing 'Prince Englebert' with 'Early Rivers'.

His son, Thomas Francis Rivers, carried on the work and next came 'Monarch' in 1885, another purple cooking plum for late September, self-fertile and early flowering. This was followed in 1901 by 'President', a variety that is no longer offered in nursery catalogues because it makes vigorous growth with very brittle branches and is self-sterile.

Laxtons also introduced a number of good plums not widely grown today. They included 'Early Laxton' (1916); 'Goldfinch' (1935), said to be from 'Early Transparent Gage' × 'Jefferson'; 'Black Prince' (1930), an early prune with damson flavour; and 'Laxton's Cropper' (1928), a late cooker said to be from 'Victoria' × 'Aylesbury Prune'.

Recommended plum and gage varieties

These are listed in approximate order of ripening and represent my selection from which I suggest reliable varieties can be chosen for a small or average-sized garden. Most are self-fertile and can therefore be planted alone. Pollination, though, is always likely to

A festooned 'Victoria' plum tree, grown on rootstock Pixy

be more fully effective where two or more are planted and this is essential where one plum is self-sterile. Over the years there has been so much in-breeding among plums and gages that certain varieties are quite unable to pollinate successfully with others. The Flowering Table on page 152 will make this clear and also lists other varieties, some with famous names which may be known to plum enthusiasts. They are omitted from my short list because of various bad points, often their over-vigorous habit or the difficulty of pollinating them, because of their early or late flowering season, or simply because they are hard to find.

Opal (Period 3) is a fairly new plum, raised in Sweden from 'Oullins Gage' × 'Early Favourite' and about the earliest self-fertile variety of dessert quality, ripening in late July and therefore possibly replacing 'Early Laxton' and 'Early Rivers', both only partially self-fertile. It has reddish-purple fruits, heavy-cropping and yellow-fleshed with almost gage-like flavour.

Czar (Period 3), raised by Thomas Rivers in 1874, is still the best early plum for culinary use, ready early August. It is a prolific and reliable bearer of juicy blue-black plums with yellow-green flesh. It forms a fairly compact, upright tree, hardy and usually frost-resistant. 'Czar' succeeds in shade and is self-fertile.

Early Transparent Gage (Period 4) was raised by Thomas Rivers in 1866, from a seed of 'Reine Claude Diaphane'. It has small to medium-sized pale yellow fruits with crimson splashes, almost transparent, and golden juicy flesh, ripening mid-August for dessert or jam. The tree makes short, stout growth and is self-fertile.

Oullins Golden Gage (Period 4) was found as a seedling at Coligny, France, and introduced in about 1860. It is a gage-plum of fairly sweet flavour with pale yellow flesh. The large round fruits are yellow with green dots, cropping well in the second half of August, and are good both for dessert and freezing. Growth is fairly vigorous and it is self-fertile and an excellent pollinator.

Denniston's Superb (Period 2) was introduced in about 1835. In the United States it was called 'Imperial Gage', having been selected at Prince's Nursery, Flushing, Long Island, from seedlings resulting from a very large sowing of 'Green Gage' stones. It is a greeny-yellow plum with green streaks, large and round. It has greengage flavour and ripens in late August, the flesh being transparent, yellow-green, and juicy. It crops heavily and makes vigorous, fairly upright growth. It is self-fertile.

Pershore Yellow Egg (Period 3) (synonyms 'Pershore Yellow', 'Yellow Egg', and 'Pershore') has golden-yellow, oval fruits of medium size with yellow flesh which make tasty jams and tarts, ripening in late August. A regular and prolific bearer, it is a hardy, well-tried, self-fertile variety.

Victoria (Period 3) is the best-known plum of all. It was found as a seedling in a garden at Alderton, Sussex, and at first named 'Sharp's Emperor'. It was sold to a nurseryman called Denyer at Brixton in 1844. He renamed it 'Denyer's Victoria' and it was quickly taken up commercially in plum-growing areas of Kent and Worcestershire and also for planting in gardens. It ripens its pale red, oval fruits in late August and early September. The flesh is greeny-yellow and of quite good flavour and it is a dual-purpose variety, good for cooking or freezing and for dessert when ripe, especially if thinned so that the fruits are of reasonable size. It can be a heavy cropper and sets well with its own pollen.

'Oullins Golden Gage'

purple-blue fruits crop freely and have yellow flesh; these are juicy and good both for cooking and, when ripe and covered in bloom, for dessert. It makes fairly vigorous, upright growth. Its self-fertile flowers come late, often missing late spring frosts.

Two less well-known plums that I have not described so far are worthy cultivars and are recommended by the Royal Horticultural Society. They are not widely grown, though, so they may be difficult to find.

Count Althann's Gage (Period 4), raised in Belgium in about 1855, was introduced by Rivers soon after that date. It is a rich, dessert gage-plum, sweet and juicy, which ripens its dark crimson fruits of medium size in late September. It makes medium growth, rather upright.

Goldfinch (Period 3) is a golden, dessert-quality plum, raised by Laxtons in 1935 from 'Early Transparent Gage' × 'Jefferson'. It ripens in mid-August, cropping heavily and hanging on well, and is of fairly compact habit. Being only partially self-fertile it needs a pollinator.

The Flowering Table on page 152 includes cultivars that are not necessarily easy to find on nurseries and are not particularly recommended for small gardens, but each has its merits.

Cambridge Gage (Period 4) a clone of the original 'Reine Claude' and also very similar to 'Old Green Gage', is ripe in late August and early September. The fruits are small, greenish-yellow with a slight red flush and the flesh is green, firm, rich, and sweet. It crops quite well and is fairly vigorous, making a compact head. It is only partially self-fertile.

Kirke's Blue (Period 4) was introduced in about 1830 by Joseph Kirke, a London nurseryman. It has large, round, dark blue plums, often thought to be the finest flavoured of all, with greenish-yellow, juicy flesh, ripening late August to mid-September. It is a somewhat shy bearer, and deserves a sunny spot and good soil. The habit is dwarfing and spreading. It must have a pollinator.

Marjorie's Seedling (Period 5) is a most useful late plum, ripening in late September and hanging on well into October. It was raised in Berkshire in 1912, but not introduced generally until 1928 and only widely distributed after 1943. Its dual-purpose, large, oval,

Opposite: 'Czar'

Belle de Louvain (Period 5) is a self-fertile Belgian variety dating from 1845 that has large, oval, reddish-purple fruits which ripen in September and cook well. It is slow to come into bearing, although prolific when it does, and makes a very vigorous tree.

Early Rivers (Period 3) is the 'Rivers Early Prolific' introduced in about 1834. It is an early cooking plum with small, dark blue fruits, ready in late July, so can be welcome for dessert if eaten when fully ripe. It is only partially self-fertile, so needs a pollinator.

Early Laxton (Period 3), introduced in 1916, is another early plum ready in late July, but golden in colour with a rosy cheek, juicy and sweet when ripe. Only partially self-fertile, it makes a small, rather weak-growing tree, somewhat susceptible to canker.

Giant Prune (Period 4) was raised by Luther Burbank in California and introduced in Britain by Bunyards of Maidstone in 1897. It has large, dark red plums with green flesh which crop regularly in mid-September, but are only of cooking quality. It does keep better than most and is self-fertile.

'Victoria'

Laxton's Cropper (Period 3), introduced in 1928, was raised by crossing 'Victoria' with 'Aylesbury Prune' and has large black, dual-purpose plums, sweet and juicy, ripening in mid-September and cropping heavily. It is self-fertile.

Ontario (Period 4) has large, golden gage-plums in late August with a gage-like flavour. It is self-fertile and sets readily. 'Ontario' makes a fairly strong and upright tree, but it is not grown commercially on many nurseries.

Pond's Seedling (Period 5) was raised before 1830 and is a cooking plum with large red fruits, good when stewed, ripening in mid-September and cropping heavily. Being self-sterile and late-flowering it needs a pollinator such as 'Marjorie's Seedling'. It makes a very vigorous tree and is, unfortunately, very liable to silver-leaf disease.

Finally, three promising new plum cultivars, with interesting pedigrees, deserve notice

Sanctus Hubertus (Period 3) is a self-sterile plum that has recently arrived in Britain from Belgium. It matures early in August and its purple-blue fruits are, for an early dessert plum, quite large. It was raised from 'Mater Dolorosa' × 'Early Rivers', its seed parent having come from 'Early Laxton' × 'Reine Claude'.

Edwards (Period 3) is a new, self-sterile plum from Oaklands, California, which has been under trial in Britain for some years and has now been taken up by a few nurseries. It ripens in mid-September. Its very large fruits are blue with purple bloom, the yellow flesh being of dessert quality, sweet and juicy.

Avalon (Period 2) is a very promising new plum from East Malling. Best described as an improved 'Victoria', it fruits eight to ten days earlier and has a very much heavier crop. 'Reeve's Seedling' was the seed parent.

'Goldfinch'

RECOMMENDED DAMSON VARIETIES

Bradley's King (Period 4) (also called 'King of Damsons') was raised by H. Bradley of Halam, Nottingham, who played a part in the introduction of 'Bramley's Seedling' apple (see page 71), and his damson was first recorded in 1880. It has prolific, medium-sized oval fruits, sweet and black when ripe and covered in a thick bloom by mid-September. It is self-fertile.

Farleigh Prolific (Period 4) (synonym 'Cluster Damson') was found growing wild in Farleigh, Kent, and it makes a sturdy, upright tree of compact habit. Being only partially self-fertile, 'Farleigh Prolific' is best pollinated by a plum to get a good crop of its small, blue-black fruits in mid-September.

Frogmore (Period 5) originated at the royal gardens at Frogmore in about 1870, and is a dual-purpose damson, ripening early. It has sweet purplish-black fruits with thick bloom and crops freely. It is only partially self-fertile.

Merryweather (Period 3) was introduced in 1907. Its origin is apparently unknown but as the blue-black fruits are bigger than other damsons it may have been the result of a cross between a plum and a damson. It bears heavily, holding its crop well through September and has strong branches that are twiggy at the extremities. It is self-fertile.

Shropshire Damson (Period 5) is sometimes called 'Prune Damson' (but also 'Westmorland Damson' or 'Cheshire Damson' in those localities). It is an old variety, known since the 17th century, and has the true damson flavour. Its medium-sized, blue-black tapering fruits hang on well through September into October. Growth is fairly upright and compact, a tidy

'Bradley's King'

habit which fits it well for the garden. This damson seems the best qualified of all the damsons to meet today's main requirements in the kitchen, including freezing. It is self-fertile.

PLUMS IN THE UNITED STATES OF AMERICA

Plums were among the first fruits to be domesticated by the early settlers in New England, as Edward Winslow recorded in 1621: 'Here are plums of three sorts, white, black and red, being almost as good as a Damson.' At least fifteen species of plums were later identified as native to the States, giving a greater divergence of fruits in size, colour, taste, and texture than any other hardy fruit. Yet American plums showed little seedling variation, a factor that had led to a marked improvement in apples, and only a few European plums had been imported by the late 1790s.

The early mission orchards of California included plums of European origin, brought from Spain through Mexico, and some survived their eventual abandonment. The Lewelling brothers brought plum trees from the eastern states to Oregon during the 1840s, and in 1856 Pierre Pellier, of San Jose, introduced plums into California for prune making in the Santa Clara Valley, which is still an important centre for this industry.

Early plums to be given names included 'Miner', grown by William Dodd in Wisconsin and distributed widely, then 'Wild Goose', found in 1820 as a stone in the crop of a goose shot by M. S. McCance on his farm at Nashville, Tennessee. John Downer then propagated it on his nursery at Elkton, Kentucky. H. A. Terry took up breeding native plums around 1857 and set up a nursery in Crescent, Iowa; his best were 'Gold', 'Hammer', 'Hawkeye', 'Downing', and 'Milton'. A plum originating in Indiana was the 'Robinson', for long popular in the Middle West and found in Putnam County about 1835.

'Shropshire Damson'

Soon, though, new varieties began to be developed, from three main sources. Firstly, there are the European plums, from *P. domestica*, which tend to be small and sweet, self-fertile and hardy. They are the easiest to dry and make into prunes. Many succeed best in the east as they need more winter chilling and ripen fruit with less heat; they thrive also in the cool Pacific Northwest. The sweetest varieties are the prune plums, with high sugar content. Secondly, there are the Japanese plums, from *P. salicina*, which are the least hardy but have bigger fruits, soft and juicy, usually eaten fresh and mostly needing pollinating. They succeed best in the west, because they need between 400 and 1,000 winter-chilling hours and the most heat to ripen fully, while their fruit buds can be killed below 0° F (18° C). Thirdly, there are the native American varieties, best for jams and other preserves. Most succeed in the upper midwest and the Canadian prairies, and on most of the continent east of the Rockies, but they have in many areas been replaced by Japanese or European plums.

The ideal soil for plums in the States is a slightly sandy, well-drained loam, pH 5.5 to 6.5; but they do not tolerate wet roots such as follows constant irrigation on lawns. Plums need to be in full sun to ripen their fruit and in areas of spring frosts it is important to ensure that cold air can drain away from their blossom. Brown rot is the major disease and requires summer spraying. Plum trees usually bear fruitfully for 12–15 years or more. Standards need 15–20 ft (4.5–6.0 m) of space, but European plums on the Nanking cherry rootstock need only 10–12 ft (3.0–3.5 m).

Recommended varieties
The plums here recommended for home gardens are listed in approximate order of ripening.

Early varieties
Methley (zones 6–10) (Japanese) originated in South

Africa. Reddish-purple plums with red flesh, not all maturing together, have excellent flavour. Pollinate with 'Burbank' or 'Shiro'.

Santa Rosa (zones 5–10) (Japanese) has deep crimson skin and pinky-yellow flesh and is good for dessert. In California, where it originated, it is an early ripener. It is self-fertile. 'Late Santa Rosa' (zones 8–9) matures six weeks later, the fruits being then sweeter and firmer. It, too, is self-fertile.

Pipestone (zones 4–8) originated in Minnesota, being bred for the coldest northern and Great Plains climates, to which it is well-suited. It has attractive red skin and sweet, juicy, yellow flesh of excellent quality. 'Superior' is a good pollinator.

Shiro (zones 5–9) (Japanese), from California, bears heavily its early, medium-large, round and clear yellow plums of good flavour. 'Methley' or 'Santa Rosa' pollinate.

Satsuma (zones 5–9) (Japanese), again from California, has small-to-medium, dark red fruits and mild red flesh with small stones. It pollinates with 'Santa Rosa'.

Mariposa (zones 6–10) (Japanese) has large heart-shaped fruit, mottled red and yellow with sweet, red, freestone flesh. From California, it is a low-chill (400 hours) plum, good in mildest climates. Pollinators are 'Santa Rosa' or 'Late Santa Rosa'.

Mid-season varieties
Burbank (zones 5–10) (Japanese) is a large red plum with excellent amber flesh; tree habit is small and drooping. Pollinate with 'Santa Rosa'.

Damson (or 'Blue Damson') (zones 5–10) is the English 'Shropshire Damson'. The tree is small and self-fertile, and it produces small fruit that is suitable for jam and cooking.

Green Gage (zones 5–9) ('Reine Claude') is cold-hardy. Greenish-yellow fruit has amber flesh with a reddish blush, of mild flavour good for dessert or preserving. The medium-sized tree is self-fertile.

Yellow Egg (zones 5–9), a fine old English plum from the Vale of Evesham, has golden fruits with yellow flesh. It is vigorous, hardy and self-fertile, best used for jam or cooking.

Stanley (zones 5–9), from New York State, has large, dark blue, freestone plums with rich yellow flesh,

tender yet firm and sweet. It bears heavily every year. It is self-fertile.

Queen Ann (zones 7–9) (Japanese) has large, freestone purple fruit with golden flesh, rich and juicy. The tree is less vigorous than others of this type. Pollinates with 'Santa Rosa'.

Ozark Premier (zones 4–8) (Japanese) bears very large, bright red fruit, yellow-fleshed and juicy with fair quality, not ripening all together. It originated in Missouri and is productive, hardy, and disease-resistant.

Late varieties
French Prune (zones 5–9) came from Europe and is the main prune variety in California, forming a large and long-lived tree. The small fruits are reddish-purple and very sweet. It is self-fertile.

Italian Prune (zones 5–9) originated in Germany and has been a popular self-fertile prune plum in the northwest. Large purple fruits have greenish flesh.

Bluefre (zones 5–7) is a productive, very large, blue freestone plum with yellow flesh, ripening late and bearing heavily on a vigorous tree, hanging on well. It came from Michigan and is a European-type, self-fertile prune plum.

President (zones 5–9) originated in England and has large blue plums with amber flesh, a useful late variety for cooking. 'Stanley' is a good pollinator.

Superior (zones 5–8) came from Minnesota and was specifically bred for the colder northern climates. It bears prolifically early in life and has large, conical red fruit with russet dots and heavily bloomed. The firm yellow flesh is good for dessert. 'Pipestone' is a good pollinator.

CULTIVATION

Plums thrive best in cultivated ground, rather than in grass, and can be incorporated in a vegetable garden, so long as the roots do not get disturbed by cultivation. They are also very suitable for growing fan-trained against a sunny wall, early flowering varieties and shy bearers needing a south-facing aspect while east- or west-facing walls are usually quite satisfactory for later-flowering varieties. The extra warmth of the wall often improves the setting of the crop as the bees prefer working there and the sun improves the sweetness. Plum trees like a reasonably heavy soil but should not be expected to grow in badly drained or waterlogged conditions, although the roots need plenty of moisture as the fruits swell over their stones. Plums dislike too much lime or chalk, but very acid soil needs dressing with lime around the roots.

Since plums come into blossom early, particularly those in flowering Periods 1 and 2, the site should be relatively free of spring frosts and not in a frost pocket. A valley or hollow, even a hedge at the bottom of a slope, can cause cold air that has drained there during a clear winter night to settle. Planting in the shade of tall trees or high buildings should also be avoided, because plums like plenty of light and sun.

In years when plums fruit well the weight can cause branches to break, particularly if rain adds to a full load. This tragedy can be avoided by thinning the fruits when quite small and by propping up the branches. If a breakage does occur the damaged surface should be trimmed and can be treated with fungicidal paint to prevent the entry of disease. It cannot be over-emphasized that plums should not be cut or pruned in winter while dormant; any training pruning should be done while the trees are in leaf between April and September.

ROOTSTOCKS

A few plums can be raised on their own roots from suckers, examples being 'Pershore Yellow Egg', 'Blaisdon Red', 'Warwickshire Drooper', 'Cambridge Gage', and some damsons. It does take a little longer to train a straight-stemmed tree from a sucker and it is usually best to cut the plant down to just above ground level at the end of its first summer after transplanting and to train a new stem up a cane. This practice is of course unnecessary if the parent tree was grafted onto a rootstock.

The rootstock most used for plums and gages is St Julien A, a virus-free clone from East Malling, which is compatible with all plum cultivars and is semi-vigorous. The more vigorous rootstock Brompton was in use where extra strong trees were needed but is now discouraged as it is thought to be more likely to succumb to plum pox, or sharka disease.

The release of the new rootstock Pixy, selected from seedlings of a French variety, 'St Julien d'Orleans', at East Malling a few years ago represented a big advance in plum growing, as it enables these fruits to be considered for quite small gardens. To succeed, Pixy needs good fertile soil and careful management, but it seldom suckers and makes a strong tree that at maturity will be only one-half to two-thirds the size of those on St Julien A. As Pixy encourages fruiting much earlier in the life of the tree, on numerous fruit spurs, it is also now possible to train plums as cordons. I have had great success with plums on Pixy using the training method known as festooning.

Damsons should be grafted on to St Julien A rootstock. I have grown 'Shropshire Damson' on Pixy, but found that it produced almost too twiggy and compact a bush.

QUINCES

Quinces probably originated in the Caucasus mountains between the Caspian and Black Seas and still grow wild in the forests of Azerbaijan in the U.S.S.R. Their species name, *Cydonia oblonga*, is derived from the city of Cydon, now Canea or Khania, in Crete, which means that they reached Greece – and, later, Italy and other parts of Europe – via that island. The fruit was dedicated both to Aphrodite and to Venus, the Greek and Roman goddesses of beauty, love, laughter, and marriage, so the fruits were eaten at nuptial ceremonies and were also used to scent the rooms. The 'golden apples' of ancient myths, such as those featured in the eleventh labour of Hercules, were probably quinces; whilst there were apples in those days they are unlikely to have been nearly so attractive as golden quinces nor to have had the same connotations.

QUINCES IN BRITAIN

Quinces may have come to Britain earlier but the first mention seems to be when Edward I planted four trees at the Tower of London in 1275, paying 6 pence each for them, about the same price as a peach tree. Seventeen years later he planted more quinces, in his gardens at Westminster, this time buying at the more favourable price of 41 shillings per hundred. There were a number of references in later centuries and the cultivation of quince trees had certainly spread to France, Spain, and Portugal by the time that John Tradescant imported quinces to Britain in 1611. In 1629 John Parkinson mentioned the single, rose-like blossom and listed six varieties. In France, nurseries along the lower end of the Loire valley were growing the Angers quince for use as rootstocks on which to graft these hybrid quinces.

The Royal Horticultural Society listed six varieties of quince in their Chiswick garden in 1826 but Robert Hogg mentioned only three in 1876 – the 'Apple-shaped', the 'Pear-shaped', and the 'Portugal'. This unhelpful nomenclature – all quinces are either apple-shaped or pear-shaped – led to misunderstandings and a lessening of interest in Britain and little, if any, hybridizing was undertaken. In the 1930s Rivers' catalogue still offered only 'Pear-shaped' and 'Portugal', while Bunyard listed 'Portugal', 'Apple-shaped', 'Bereczeki', and 'Vranja' – the latter

two varieties having been imported from Serbia (Yugoslavia) between the two world wars. Quinces were never popular for eating raw and interest in them was overtaken by the arrival of other soft fruits.

In recent years there has been a rediscovery of these traditional fruits for their decorative value and ease of culture in gardens and for jam making. They are all self-fertile and present few problems to the home gardener.

Recommended varieties
Vranja, the quince I grow in my own garden, does well given a good loamy soil with plenty of moisture. The leaves are large, leathery, dark green, woolly on the undersides and generally disease-resistant. The flowers are 2 in (5 cm) wide with a very attractive pink tinge and a delicate fragrance. The fruits are pear-shaped,

'Portugal'

'Portugal'

large and handsome, pale gold in colour as they ripen, becoming covered in white, cotton-like, short hairs.

Bereczki, named after an eminent Hungarian pomologist, is so similar to 'Vranja' as to be virtually the same plant.

Champion has large, round, greeny-yellow apple-shaped fruits of very delicate flavour; it fruits well when still young.

Meech's Prolific was raised in Connecticut by the Reverend W. Meech, before 1850, and is distributed in the United States under the name 'Orange Quince', of which it was a seedling. It has large flowers and bears bright, golden-yellow, pear-shaped fruits with smooth skins and excellent flavour. It is earlier than 'Vranja' and crops well when still young. It makes a vigorous, although slow- growing, tree.

Portugal (syn. 'Lusitanica') was imported by John Tradescant in 1611 for Lord Burleigh. It makes a tall, vigorous tree, somewhat shy-bearing, having large, oblong, pear-shaped, mild-flavoured fruits. These are green, ripening to pale orange, which turns red when cooked. A less hardy variety, it is best suited to warmer areas.

QUINCES IN THE UNITED STATES OF AMERICA

Quinces were taken to America from Europe by some of its earliest colonists and for a time the gnarled trees were commonly grown. But quinces fell out of favour — they were used only to make quince jelly or as a minor ingredient in a fruitcake. In 19th-century slang, 'quince' means an unpleasant, sour-tongued woman.

Recommended varieties
Only three cultivars are recognized for home gardens

and they succeed wherever winter temperatures do not drop below $-15°F$ ($-26°C$) and generally in zones 5–10.

Orange, sometimes called 'Apple Quince', takes its name from the colour of its flesh. It is believed to have originated in southern Europe; fruits are usually apple-shaped, but variable.

Pineapple originated in California and is rounded in shape with white, rather tender flesh and a taste resembling the pineapple. It can be cooked without the addition of water.

Smyrna originated in Turkey and has the largest fruits of the three. It is somewhat elongated in shape, with yellow flesh and a strong quince fragrance.

CULTIVATION

The quince tree is an excellent choice for a smallish garden because it fruits early in its life and is fairly slow-growing and it does not cast much shade, being upright and compact in habit. Quinces can be grown as open-centred bushes, half standards, or cordons or fan-trained on walls. As they flower a little later than pears, quince trees are less likely to be damaged by late frosts. The blossom sets a better crop if the trees are planted in a spot sheltered from cold winds. Quinces are self-fertile and have few pests or diseases to worry them, plenty of moisture in dry spells being their main need.

The quince is normally grafted on Quince A rootstock. This is of medium vigour, like MM.106 for apples. The slightly dwarfer rootstock, Quince C, is a possible alternative where the soil conditions are particularly good.

Quinces should be left to remain on the tree for as long as possible; in Britain they are best picked in late October, before the onset of severe frosts.

Because quinces have a strong, spicy scent, they should be stored separately from other fruits, which otherwise can pick up the quince scent and have their flavour spoilt.

WALNUTS

The walnut is probably native to the Himalayas. It was grown in Persia for several thousand years and carried westward through Asia Minor to Greece and to Rome. The generic part of the Latin name for the common walnut, *Juglans regia*, is a contraction of *Jovis glans*, which means Jove's, or Jupiter's, nut – the implication being that the common man ate acorns or hazelnuts while the gods enjoyed walnuts. In the first century A.D. Pliny the Elder wrote about walnuts – as he did about most fruits – noting the medicines and dyes that could be made from the shells and from the young nuts.

A walnut tree

WALNUTS IN BRITAIN

The Romans in Britain used walnuts both for eating and as a source of cooking oil, but their nuts were probably imported, as there is no evidence of trees growing in Britain then. By the 14th century, though, trees seem to have reached Britain from Europe. In 1358 Durham Priory sold its walnuts for 15 pence a thousand and these must surely have come from the priory's own trees. Henry VIII was probably responsible for introducing better-fruiting clones, and by the end of the 16th century walnuts were fairly widely planted, in fields, orchards, and the larger private gardens belonging to the rich.

Opposite: walnut husks. Above: a very old walnut tree

There are numerous examples of the common walnut growing around Britain and young trees can be bought from fruit-tree nurseries. But anyone planting now might be advised to give the space to a grafted cultivar, which should fruit more reliably and sooner in life and bear tastier nuts. Two are becoming available from English growers, albeit in small numbers because of the difficulty of getting sufficient of the grafts to take.

The problem is two-fold – to get the scion wood from the chosen mother tree in sufficient numbers and of exactly the right size and ripeness and to get sufficient suitable rootstocks of just the right size and age to match the graft-wood. Also, even highly skilled grafters find that while they can get some grafts to take one year, next year the same operation can fail.

Recommended varieties

Buccaneer, a hybrid from Russia and therefore used to colder climes, is self-fertile and produces regularly a good, heavy crop of high-quality nuts that are borne on quite young trees.

Broadview, from Germany, is another hybrid that crops equally well but is not self-fertile and needs a pollinator; 'Buccaneer' will serve.

Franquette is a clone from the Isère department of France, named after its raiser. It flowers a little later than the common walnut and is more likely to miss late frosts. It bears large nuts early in life if pollinated.

Mayott is another late-flowering French cultivar that ripens a little later than 'Franquette'.

WALNUTS IN THE UNITED STATES OF AMERICA

The black walnut (*J. nigra*) is a prized hardwood, native to the eastern and central United States, and a lovely shade tree where space allows. For the home garden there is a grafted variety called 'Thomas', selected in Pennsylvania, which is hardy and an abundant cropper, bearing thin-shelled nuts only two or three years after planting. This grows to about 60 ft (18 m) and needs to be pollinated by another black walnut, either a seedling or a grafted tree such as 'Stark Kwik-Krop' or 'Stabler', both selected fruiting cultivars. All three grow in zones 5–8.

The butternut (*J. cinerea*) is a native of the northeastern United States and south-east Canada, often found on stream banks or roadsides where the soil is rich and well drained. It is smaller than the black walnut, with light grey bark that breaks into elongated ridges. The edible nuts are long and pointed, in green, gummy husks.

J. regia is known in the United States as the English or Persian walnut. It is fast-growing to about 60 ft (18 m) high and wide. For home gardens it is best to choose a smaller, grafted cultivar, which will bear superior-tasting fruits. Some of these cultivars are self-fertile, but most fruit much more reliably if planted near a pollinator – any English walnut will serve.

Recommended varieties

For the midwestern and eastern states, where winter lows are normally between −20°F (−29°C) and −30°F (−34°C), the Carpathian group of English walnuts often succeed best. For zones 6–8:

Broadview has been found to be best for Texas.
Colby has adapted well north of the Ohio River.
Lake, which makes a smaller tree than these, is good in Illinois and Missouri.
Adams and **Mesa** are other less well-known Carpathians worth trying.

Other (non-Carpathian) varieties of English walnut have proved their worth in the less cold parts of the midwestern and eastern states in zones 6–7.

Hansen, a smaller, self-fertile tree from Ohio, leafs in mid-season and bears thin-shelled nuts.
McKinster, from Ohio, leafs late and is self-fertile.
Metcalfe leafs late and is productive in New York State.
Somers comes from Michigan and ripens very early, so is good in short-season districts; it is also resistant to husk fly.
Stark Champion comes from Missouri and makes a smaller tree, quick to fruit when pollinated.

A number of English walnut cultivars do well in the western states. Most originated in California and succeed in zones 8 and 9.

Carmelo leafs late, bears large nuts, and resists sun burn.
Chandler leafs mid-late and bears quality nuts. 'Hartley' or 'Franquette' pollinate.
Chico leafs early and makes a smaller tree; best with hard pruning, it is a good pollinator for most others.
Concord leafs mid-late and is best in the milder coastal region.
Franquette, from France, leafs late and has adapted well to the late springs of the northwest, but it is not a heavy cropper. 'Chandler' or 'Hartley' pollinate.
Hartley leafs mid-season and bears good-quality nuts early in life. It is self-fertile, or 'Franquette' will pollinate.
Howard leafs mid-season and makes a smaller but heavy-bearing tree. 'Hartley' or 'Franquette' pollinate.
Placentia leafs early and is self-fertile, bearing young. As it needs little winter chill it is good in southern California.

CULTIVATION

Although quite fast-growing when young the common walnut can take up to ten years to start setting fruit. In May it bears male catkins of numerous flowers on one-year-old twigs while female flowers grow in groups of two to four at the tips of the new shoots, all on the same tree. These are neither conspicuous nor scented and are not used to attract insects because walnuts are wind-pollinated. It follows that dry weather is needed as the pollen ripens, so that it can be wind blown, and that at the same time the female flowers on the little nutlets must be ready to receive it. These three factors do not always coincide and this can account for a failure to fruit in some years, more particularly with young trees. Where two or more walnuts are near, regular success is more probable.

A tree that comes into leaf late, say in mid-May, stands the best chance of its young shoots and catkins missing late frosts, to which they are susceptible below about 27°F (−3°C). It is important not to plant a walnut in a frost pocket and if a site can be chosen that is sheltered from the north and east winds good pollination is much more likely.

Common walnuts can reach 60 ft (18 m) in height when growing in a suitably deep, well-drained soil and they have silvery bark, smooth on young trees but becoming deeply fissured with age. Usually grown as standard or half-standard trees with central leaders, walnuts are best planted young, as they resent root disturbance. Buy a tree perhaps 5–6 ft (1.5–1.8 m) in height and 3 years old with some branches near the top and plant it against a stake to which it can be tied or strapped. Very little pruning is required once the head is formed, but if dead or awkwardly placed branches need to be cut out this is done in August while the trees are in leaf. Any wounds should be painted over, in order to avoid bleeding of the sap.

If there is room for only one tree be sure to choose a self-fertile cultivar. As walnuts are long-lived their eventual size should be remembered when planting and a site chosen with good, deep, well-drained soil, preferably of pH 6 to 6.5. Although they are tolerant of drought they like deep watering when the nuts are being formed. They dislike, though, having the base of the trunk saturated, as may happen when lawn sprinklers are used. A basin can be formed under the spread of the tree's canopy, starting a foot or so out from the trunk, to be filled with water when a good soak is wanted.

Walnuts are attacked by few pests or diseases – which may be one reason why they are long-lived. In some areas, rooks and squirrels steal the fruits while they are still soft – that is, at the ideal stage for man to take them for pickling. The problem most likely to be encountered is bacterial blight; it causes black spots on the leaves, distortion of the leaflets, and black sunken lesions on the nuts. The bacteria overwinter on the one-year-old shoots and on the bud scales, being spread in spring and summer by rain and mists. The treatment is to spray with Bordeaux mixture in mid-June and again in July. Leaves showing the typical blotches should be gathered in autumn and burnt. Young trees may also be attacked by aphids, which may be controlled by insecticide sprays. In the western United States the walnut husk fly sometimes attacks orchards.

HARVESTING AND STORING

The best way to harvest walnuts is to pick them off the ground as soon as they fall and to de-husk them immediately – if the husks are left on they turn black and become difficult to remove. The fruit of the walnut is technically a drupe or stone-fruit, like the cherry, the nut being the equivalent of the cherry's stone. The outer layer is a round body, somewhat like a coarse-skinned plum, green at first until the thick flesh turns brown and rots as the fruit ripens in late September.

In order to ensure that the nuts keep in good condition for eating when freed from their outer layers they are then dipped in water and scrubbed hard to remove the fibres; it is here that moulds begin to grow. They are then spread out in a warm place to dry and turned every few days before being packed into jars between layers of equal parts dry peat and sand with some salt added. The jars are stood in a cool, frost-free place and should keep the nuts in good condition for at least 6 months.

APPENDIX 1: APPLE IDENTIFICATION TABLE

Group I: smooth-skinned, green, sour culinary apples

Season	Flat	Round	Conical	Oblong
August		Grenadier	Early Victoria	
September	Stirling Castle	Potts' Seedling	Lord Grosvenor	
October	Ecklinville	Charles Eyre		
November			Lord Derby Shoesmith	
December	Broad-Eyed Pippin		Warner's King	Catshead
January		Dewdney's Seedling		
February		Edward VII Hormead Pearmain Woolbrook Russet	Rhode Island Greening	Alfriston Gloria Mundi
March				
April		French Crab		Gooseberry

Group II: smooth-skinned, green, sweet dessert apples

Season	Flat	Round	Conical	Oblong
January		Bascombe Mystery		
February		Newtown Pippin		
March		Granny Smith		Sturmer Pippin

Group III: striped, smooth-skinned, sour culinary apples

Season	Flat	Round	Conical	Oblong
September	Queen	George Neal		
October		Frogmore Prolific Bountiful	Alexander Tom Putt	
November		Bushey Grove Cox's Pomona		
December		Monarch	Isaac Newton's Tree Horneburger Pfannkuchen Loddington	
January	Belle de Pontoise Bramley's Seedling	Arthur W. Barnes Byfleet Seedling Chelmsford Wonder Cottenham Seedling Newton Wonder Yorkshire Greening	Beauty of Kent Bismarck Lane's Prince Albert Lewis's Incomparable Smart's Prince Arthur	
February	Dumelow's Seedling Ontario	Crawley Beauty	Howgate Wonder Northern Greening	Annie Elizabeth Encore
March		Striped Beefing		

Group IV: smooth-skinned, flushed or striped, sweet dessert apples

Season	Flat	Round	Conical	Oblong
August	Beauty of Bath Exeter Cross Owen Thomas	Advance George Cave	Irish Peach Lady Sudeley Melba	Close Duchess of Oldenburg
September	Maidstone Favourite	Miller's Seedling Bolero	Baker's Delicious Cheddar Cross James Grieve	Benoni
October		Wealthy	Forge	
November	Cambusnethan Pippin	Cellini Chorister Boy Coronation Hoary Morning Peasgood's Nonsuch Rival	Charles Ross Washington Strawberry Rubinette	Gravenstein
December		Chivers Delight Telstar	Falstaff	
January		Rome Beauty	Joybells King of Tompkins County	Spigold
February	Wagener	Dutch Mignonne King George V	Upton Pyne	Delicious
March				
April			Hambledon Deux Ans	

Group V: yellow-skinned dessert and culinary apples

Season	Flat	Round	Conical	Oblong
August			Lodi[1] Lord Suffield[1] White Transparent	
September			Keswick Codlin[1] Reverend W. Wilks[1]	
October			Arthur Turner[1] Carlisle Codling[1]	Greensleeves
November		Burr Knot[1] Curl Tail[1] Freyburg Galloway Pippin[1] Golden Noble[1] Norfolk Beauty[1]	Alderman[1] Royal Jubilee[1]	Histon Favourite
December			Cleopatra Harvey[1] Landsberger Reinette	
January		Wyken Pippin	Calville Blanc d'Hiver[2] High View Pippin Lemon Pippin[1] Winter Banana	Crispin Golden Delicious Grimes Golden
February		Boiken		Bedfordshire Foundling[1] Eady's Magnum[1]

[1] Culinary
[2] Dual-purpose

Group VI: mainly red, mainly dessert apples

Season	Flat	Round	Conical	Oblong
August	Devonshire Quarrenden Discovery	Red Astrachan Stark's Earliest	Gladstone Langley Pippin	
September	Ben's Red Duchess's Favourite Redsleeves	Merton Beauty Merton Knave Tydeman's Early Worcester	Crimson Queening Katy Merton Worcester Worcester Pearmain	
October		Polka Waltz	Herring's Pippin Summerred	
November	Guelph	Cortland Fameuse Gascoyne's Scarlet[2] Ingrid Marie Lobo McIntosh Michaelmas Red Reinette Rouge Etoilée Wolf River[1]	Millicent Barnes Mother Norfolk Royal	Madresfield Court
December	Herefordshire Beefing	Baumann's Reinette[2] Spartan	Beauty of Hants	Gala Jonathan Spencer
January	Mère de Ménage[1]	Baxter's Pearmain	Blue Pearmain[2] Cornish Aromatic Northern Spy Star of Devon William Crump	Calville Rouge d'Hiver[1]
February		Baldwin John Standish Jonagold Norfolk Beefing[1]	Melrose	Gloster 69
March	Idared	Democrat		

[1] Culinary
[2] Dual-purpose

Group VII: reinettes, skin coloured with some russet dessert apples

Season	Flat	Round	Conical	Oblong
September		Beeley Pippin Epicure Merton Charm Saint Everard	Exquisite Fortune Kerry Pippin Merton Joy	
October		Ellison's Orange Lord Lambourne Jester	Autumn Pearmain Pearl	
November		Sunset Fiesta	Elstar Allington Pippin Carswell's Orange Margil Jupiter	George Carpenter King of the Pippins
December		Blenheim Orange[2] Houblon Orleans Reinette Ross Nonpareil Saltcote Pippin	Ard Cairn Russet Christmas Pearmain Cox's Orange Pippin Holstein Kidd's Orange Red Mabbott's Pearmain Ribston Pippin	Lady Henniker

[1] Culinary
[2] Dual-purpose

Group VII (continued)

Season	Flat	Round	Conical	Oblong

January	Fearn's Pippin
	Heusgen's Golden
	  Reinette
		Barnack Orange
		Suntan
			Bess Pool
			Claygate Pearmain
			Laxton's Superb
			Mannington's
			  Pearmain
			Rosemary Russet
			Saint Cecilia
				Adams's Pearmain
				Barnack Beauty
				Bow Hill Pippin
				Cornish Gillyflower
				Roundway Magnum
				  Bonum[2]

February	Court Pendu Plat Pixie	Lord Burghley	Belle de Boskoop[2] Kent King's Acre Pippin Lord Hindlip Tydeman's Late Orange Winston	
March	Allen's Everlasting			
April	May Queen			

[1] Culinary
[2] Dual-purpose

Group VIII: skin mainly russet dessert apples

Season	Flat	Round	Conical	Oblong
October		Saint Edmund's Pippin		
November		Egremont Russet	Norfolk Royal Russet	Pitmaston Pine Apple
December				
January		Ashmead's Kernel Nonpareil	Cockle Pippin Zabergäu Renette	Pine Golden Pippin
February		Brownlees' Russet Duke of Devonshire	Nutmeg Pippin Reinette du Canada	D'Arcy Spice

APPENDIX 2:
FLOWERING TABLES

FLOWERING OF APPLES

Group 1: very early
Bolero
Gravenstein (T)
Lord Suffield
Mank's Codling (B)
Polka
Red Astrachan
Stark Earliest (syn. Scarlet Pimpernel)

Group 2
Acme
Adam's Pearmain (B)
Baker's Delicious
Beauty of Bath
Beauty of Blackmoor
Ben's Red (B)
Bismarck (B)
Cheddar Cross
Christmas Pearmain (B)
Devonshire Quarrrenden (B)
Egremont Russet
George Cave
George Neal
Golden Spire
Idared
Irish Peach
Kerry Pippin
Keswick Codling (B)
Laxton's Early Crimson
Lord Lambourne
Margil
McIntosh Red
Melba (B)
Merton Charm
Michaelmas Red
Norfolk Beauty
Owen Thomas
Rev. W. Wilks (B)
Ribston Pippin (T)
Ross Nonpareil
St Edmund's Pippin
Striped Beefing
Vistabella (B)
Warner's King (T)
Washington (T)
White Transparent

Group 3
Acme
Allington Pippin (B)
Arthur Turner
Barnack Orange
Baumann's Reinette (B)
Belle de Boskoop (T)
Belle de Pontoise (B)
Blenheim Orange (TB)
Bountiful
Bowden's Seedling
Bramley's Seedling (T)
Brownlee's Russet
Charles Ross
Cox's Orange Pippin
Crispin (T)
Discovery
Duchess Favourite
Elstar
Emperor Alexander
Emneth Early (Early Victoria (B)
Epicure
Exeter Cross
Exquisite
Falstaff
Feltham Beauty
Fiesta
Fortuna (B)
Gavin
Goldilocks
Granny Smith
Greensleeves
Grenadier
Hambling's Seedling
Holstein (T)
Hormead Pearmain
James Grieve
John Standish
Jonagold (T)
Jonathan
Jupiter (T)
Karmijn de Sonnaville (T)
Katy (Katja)
Kidd's Orange Red
King of Tompkins County (T)
King Russet
Lane's Prince Albert

Langley Pippin
Lord Grosvenor
Lord Hindlip
Malling Kent
Mère de Ménage
Merton Knave
Merton Prolific
Merton Russet
Merton Worcester
Miller's Seedling (B)
New Hawthornden
Norfolk Royal Russet
Ontario
Peasgood's Nonsuch
Queen
Red Victoria (B)
Redsleeves
Reinette du Canada (T)
Rival (B)
Rosemary Russet
Rubinette
St Cecilia
St Everard
Spartan
Stirling Castle
Sturmer Pippin
Sunset
Taunton Cross
Tom Putt
Tydeman's Early Worcester
Wagener (B)
Waltz
Wealthy
Worcester Pearmain
S.T. Wright
Wyken Pippin

Group 4
Annie Elizabeth
Ashmead's Kernel
Autumn Pearmain
Barnack Beauty
Chivers' Delight
Claygate Pearmain
Cornish Gillyflower
Cox's Pomona
D'Arcy Spice
Delicious
Duke of Devonshire
Dumelow's Seedling (Wellington)
Ellison's Orange
Encore
Gala
George Carpenter
Gladstone (B)
Gloster 69
Golden Delicious
Golden Noble
Hawthornden
Herring's Pippin
Howgate Wonder
Ingrid Marie
Jester
Joybells
King's Acre Pippin
Lady Henniker
Lady Sudeley
Laxton's Pearmain
Lord Derby
Mannington's Pearmain
Monarch (B)
Orleans Reinette
Pixie
Sir John Thornycroft
Laxton's Superb (B)
Tydeman's Late Orange
Winston
Woolbrook Russet
Yellow Newtown (B)

Group 5
Coronation (B)
Gascoyne's Scarlet (T)
King of the Pippins (B)
Merton Beauty
Mother (American)
Newton Wonder
Northern Spy (B)
Reinette Rouge Etoilée
Royal Jubilee
Suntan (T)
William Crump
Woolbrook Pippin (B)

Group 6
Bess Pool
Court Pendu Plat
Edward VII

Group 7: very late
Crawley Beauty

B = Known to be biennial or irregular in flowering
T = Triploid
Colour sports usually flower at the same time as the cultivar from which they originated. The following combinations are incompatible: 'Cox's Orange Pippin' pollinated by 'Kidd's Orange Red' and the reverse; 'Cox's Orange Pippin' is ineffective on 'Holstein' and 'Suntan', and the reverse; 'Golden Delicious' may be ineffective on 'Crispin' ('Mutsu'). With these exceptions, apples cross-pollinate with others in the same flowering group. They also partially overlap with other cultivars in adjacent groups, for example Group 2 overlaps with Group 3, and 3 with 4.

FLOWERING OF CHERRIES

	Flowering period 1 (earliest)	Flowering period 2	Flowering period 3	Flowering period 4	Flowering period 5	Flowering period 6 (latest)
Universal donors	Noir de Guben Nutberry Black	Merton Glory Merchant		Summit	Bigarreau Gaucher Florence	
Incompatibility group 1	Early Rivers	Bedford Prolific Knight's Early Black	Roundel Heart			
Incompatibility group 2		Bigarreau de Schrecken Mermat Merton Favourite Waterloo	Frogmore Early Merton Bigarreau Merton Bounty Van	Belle Agathe Merton Crane		
Incompatibility group 3			Merton Marvel	Emperor Francis Napoleon Bigarreau		
Incompatibility group 4			Merton Premier	Kent Bigarreau		
Incompatibility group 5					Late Black Bigarreau	
Incompatibility group 6		Merton Heart	Early Amber Elton Heart Governor Wood			
Incompatibility group 7						Bradbourne Black Géante d'Hedelfinger
Incompatibility group 8			Peggy Rivers			
Incompatibility group 9				Merton Reward	Merton Late	
Self-compatible		Lapins May Duke	Stella Sunburst	Morello		

The six universal donors will cross-pollinate with any cherry in the Flowering-period column below them, as well as those in adjacent columns.

The five self-compatible (i.e., self-fertile) cherries will pollinate themselves and others in the vertical columns above them and in the adjacent columns.

No two cherries in the same incompatibility group will cross-pollinate one another. For example, 'Van' will not cross-pollinate with any cherries in Group 2 but will with 'Roundel' and others in Flowering period 3, also with those in vertical columns 2 and 4.

The flowering period is not an accurate indication of the fruiting season; see descriptions in the text for this.

FLOWERING OF PEARS

Group 1: very early	**Group 2: early**	**Group 3: mid-period**	**Group 4: Late**
Brockworth Park	Baronne de Mello	Belle-Julie	Beth
Maréchal de la Cour (T)	Bellissime d'Hiver	Beurré Dumont	Beurré Bedford (MS)
Précoce de Trévoux	Beurré Alexandre Lucas (T)	Beurré Hardy	Beurré Mortillet
	Beurré d'Amanlis (T)	Beurré Superfin	Bristol Cross (MS)
	Beurré d'Anjou	Black Worcester	Calebasse Bosc
	Beurré Clairgeau	Conference	Catillac (T)
	Beurré Diel (T)	Doyenné Boussoch (T)	Clapp's Favourite
	Beurré Giffard	Doyenné George Boucher	Concorde
	Beurré Six	Dr Jules Guyot	Doyenné du Comice
	Comtesse de Paris	Duchesse de Bordeaux	Glou Morceau
	Doyenné d'Eté	Durondeau	Gorham
	Duchesse d'Angoulême	Fertility	Improved Fertility

T = triploid   MS = male sterile

Table continued overleaf

FLOWERING OF PEARS (continued)

Group 1: very early	Group 2: early	Group 3: mid-period	Group 4: Late
	Easter Beurré	Fondante d'Automne	Laxton's Foremost
	Emile d'Heyst	Fondante Thirriott	Laxton's Victor
	Louise Bonne of Jersey	Hessle	Marie Louise
	Marguerite Marillat (MS)	Jargonelle (T)	Napoleon
	Packham's Triumph	Josephine de Malines	Nouveau Poiteau
	Passe Crasanne	Laxton's Early Market	Onward
	Princess	Laxton's Progress	Pitmaston Duchess (T)
	Seckel	Laxton's Satisfaction	Santa Claus
	St Luke	Le Lectier	Winter Nelis
	Uvedale's St Germain (T)	Merton Pride (T)	Zépherin Grégoire
	Vicar of Winkfield (T)	Nouvelle Fulvie	
		Olivier de Serres	
		Roosevelt	
		Souvenir du Congrés	
		Thompson's	
		Triomphe de Vienne	
		Williams' Bon Chrétien	

T = triploid   MS = male sterile

Very few fruits will be produced from self-pollination, except for 'Improved Fertility' and seedless pears of 'Conference'.

To ensure cross-pollination, choose two or more pears from the same group or one adjoining; i.e., pears in Group 2 cross-pollinate with, for preference, others in Group 2 but also with those in Groups 1 and 3. Pears in Group 4 cross-pollinate not only with others in Group 4 but also with those in Group 3.

The following pears are incompatible: 'Beurré d'Amanlis' with 'Conference' and 'Doyenné du Comice' with 'Onward'.

The following pears are all incompatible with each other: 'Fondante d'Automne', 'Laxton's Progress', 'Louise Bonne of Jersey', 'Précoce de Trévoux', 'Seckle', and 'Williams' Bon Chrétien'.

Triploid and male-sterile pears are ineffective as pollinators for others, so two other pears are required, to pollinate both themselves and the triploid or male-sterile cultivar.

FLOWERING OF PLUMS, GAGES, AND DAMSONS

	Flowering period 1 (early)	Flowering period 2	Flowering period 3	Flowering period 4	Flowering period 5
Compatibility Group A (self-sterile)	Jefferson	Coe's Golden Drop President	Bryanston Gage Reeves Seedling Sanctus Hubertus Washington	Count Althann's Gage Kirke's Blue	Frogmore Damson Late Transparent Old Green Gage Pond's Seedling
Compatibility Group B (partially self-fertile)	Angelina Burdett	Curlew	Early Laxton Early Rivers Edwards Goldfinch	Cambridge Gage Farleigh Prolific Damson	
Compatibility Group C (self-fertile)	Monarch	Avalon Denniston's Superb Reine-Claude de Bavay Warwickshire Drooper	Czar Laxton's Cropper Laxton's Supreme Merryweather Damson Opal Pershore Yellow Egg Purple Pershore Thames Cross Victoria	Blaisdon Red Bradley's King Damson Early Transparent Gage Giant Prune Ontario Oullins Golden Gage	Belle de Louvain Marjorie's Seedling Prune Damson

Each Flowering period lasts four days. Trees in Group C will set fruit with their own blossom and can stand alone. Trees in Groups A and B are self-sterile and must be pollinated by another plum from the same Flowering-period column or from one of the two adjacent columns. 'Jefferson' and 'Coe's Golden Drop' however, will not pollinate each other and 'Cambridge Gage' and 'Old Green Gage' should not be used to pollinate each other because the result will be very poor.

Some Gardens to Visit

United Kingdom

Barrington Court Gardens, Ilminster, Somerset

Castle Bromwich Hall Gardens Trust, Chester Road, Castle Bromwich, West Midlands

Clumber Park, nr Worksop, Nottinghamshire

Croxteth Hall and Country Park, Liverpool, Merseyside

East Riddlesden Hall, Keighley, West Yorkshire

Erdigg, nr Wrexham, Clwyd

Harlow Car Gardens, Crag Lane, Harrogate, North Yorkshire

Painswick Rococo Garden, Painswick, Gloucestershire

Parceval Hall Gardens, Burnsall, North Yorkshire

Priorwood Garden, Melrose, Borders

Tapeley Park, Instow, Devon

Westbury Court Garden, Westbury-on-Severn, Gloucestershire

Wisley Garden (Royal Horticultural Society), Wisley, Woking, Surrey

United States of America

Delaware

The Nemours Foundation, Rockland Road off Route 141, Wilmington

District of Columbia

U.S. National Arboretum, 24th & R Streets N.E., Washington

Kentucky

Farmington Historic Home Museum, 3033 Bardstown Road, Louisville

Massachusetts

Berkshire Garden Center, Junction Routes 102 & 183, Stockbridge

Mississippi

Wister Henry Garden, Route 7, Belzoni

New Jersey

Deep Cut Park Horticultural Center, Newman Springs Road, Middletown

New York

Boscobel Restoration, Route 9D, Garrison-on-Hudson

North Carolina

Elizabethan Gardens, Fort Raleigh National Historic Site, Manteo

Tyron Palace Restoration, George & Pollock Streets, New Bern

Orton Plantation, Route 133, Winabow

Pennsylvania

Ambler Campus, Temple University, Ambler

Utah

Utah Botanical Gardens, 1817 North Main Street, Farmington

Virginia

River Farm (American Horticultural Society), 7931 East Boulevard Drive, Alexandria

Mount Vernon, Mount Vernon Memorial Highway, Mount Vernon

Colonial Williamsburg, Williamsburg

Wisconsin

Alfred L. Boerner Botanical Gardens, 5879 South 92nd Street, Hales Corner

NURSERIES

United Kingdom

J. C. Allgrove Ltd, The Nursery, Middle Green,
    Langley, Buckinghamshire

Bees of Chester, Sealand Nurseries Ltd, Sealand,
    Chester, Cheshire CH1 6BA

Chris. Bowers & Sons, Whispering Trees Nurseries,
    Wimbotsham, Norfolk PE34 8QB

Bridgemere Nurseries Ltd, Bridgemere, Nantwich,
    Cheshire CW5 7QB

Cornish Garden Nurseries Ltd, Peran-ar-Worthal,
    Truro, Cornwall TR3 7PE

Dayspring Nursery, Quarr, Buckthorn Weston,
    Gillingham, Dorset SP8 5PA

Deacons Nursery, Moor View, Godshill, Isle of Wight
    PO38 3HW

Eden Nurseries, Rectory Lane, Old Bolingbroke,
    Spilsby, Lincolnshire

Family Trees (Philip House), Summerlands, Curdridge,
    Botley, Hampshire SO3 2DS

Highfield Nurseries, Whitminster, Gloucester
    GL2 7PL

Hillier Nurseries Ltd, Ampfield House, Ampfield,
    Romsey, Hampshire SO5 9PA

Keepers Nursery, 446 Wateringbury Road, East
    Malling, Maidstone, Kent ME19 6JJ

Frank P. Matthews Ltd, Berrington Court, Tenbury
    Wells, Worcestershire WR15 8TH

Matthews Fruit Trees Ltd, Thurston, Bury
    St Edmunds, Suffolk IP31 3RN

New Tree Nurseries, 2 Nunnery Road, Canterbury,
    Kent CT1 3LS

Notcutt's Nurseries Ltd, Woodbridge, Suffolk
    IP12 4AF

Read's Nursery, Hales Hall, Loddon, Norfolk
    NR14 6QW

A. E. Roberts Ltd, Frith Farm, Wickham, Fareham,
    Hampshire PO17 5AW

R. V. Roger Ltd, The Nurseries, Pickering, North
    Yorkshire YO18 7HG

St Bridget Nurseries Ltd, Old Rydon Lane, Exeter,
    Devon EX2 7JY

Scott's Nurseries Ltd, Merriott, Somerset TA16 5PL

J. Tweedie Fruit Trees, 504 Denby Dale Road West,
    Calder Grove, Wakefield, West Yorkshire WF4 3DB

United States of America

Adams County Nursery, Box 108, Aspers,
    Pennsylvania 17304

Bear Creek Nursery, Box 411, Northport, Washington
    99157

Bountiful Ridge Nurseries, Inc., Box 250, Princess
    Anne, Maryland 21853

Columbia Basin Nursery, Box 458, Quincy,
    Washington 98848

Cumberland Valley Nurseries, Inc., Box 471,
    McMinnville, Tennessee 37110

Emlong Nurseries, 2671 W. Marquette Woods Road,
    Stevensville, Michigan 49127

Fowler Nurseries, Inc., 525 Fowler Road, Newcastle,
    California 95658

Hilltop Orchards & Nurseries, Inc., Route 2, Hartford,
    Michigan 49057

Lawson's Nursery, Route 1, Box 294, Ball Ground,
    Georgia 30107

Henry Leuthart Nurseries, Inc., Box 666, Montauk
    Highway, East Moriches, New York 11940

Living Tree Center, Box 797, Bolinas, California 94914

Mayo Nurseries, 8393 Klippel Road, Lyons, New York
    14489

J. E. Miller Nurseries, 5060 West Lake Road,
    Canandaigua, New York 14424

New York State Fruit Testing Cooperative Association,
    Box 462, Geneva, New York 14456

Patrick's Nursery, Box 130, Ty Ty, Georgia 31795

Preservation Apple Tree Company, Box 607, Mount
    Gretna, Pennsylvania 17064

Raintree Nursery, 391 Butts Road, Morton,
    Washington 98356

Rayner Brothers, Box 1717, Salisbury, Maryland 21801

St Lawrence Nurseries, RD2, Potsdam, New York
    13676

Southmeadow Fruit Gardens, 15310 Red Arrow
    Highway, Lakeside, Michigan 49116

Stark Brothers Nursery, Highway 54 West, Louisiana,
    Missouri 63353

Van Well Nursery, Box 1339, Wenatchee, Washington
    98801

Waynesboro Nurseries, Box 987, Waynesboro,
    Virginia 22980

GLOSSARY

Biennial bearers flower and fruit only in alternate years. This habit can be partly controlled by removing at least half the fruit buds in the 'on' year and feeding the tree so that it can both crop this year and make new fruit buds for next year.

Bridge grafting is done when animals have eaten the bark around a tree, the scion being united above and below the damage.

Clone describes a plant genetically uniform with its parent, produced by vegetative propagation, not from seed, and from one original ancestor or its vegetatively produced offspring.

Compatibility means the ability of cultivars to cross-pollinate each other. Those that cannot do so are said to be incompatible.

Crinkle-crankle describes a wall in a fruit garden, built in serpentine fashion without buttresses, to provide sheltered, sunny positions for trained fruit trees.

Diploid apples and pears – the majority – have two sets of 17 chromosomes (34) in their make-up, the normal number. Triploids have three sets (51); these are very poor pollinators and also make larger trees than diploids.

Drupes are fruits having an outer skin, a fleshy layer, and a hard stone protecting the seed inside. Apricots, cherries, nectarines, peaches, and plums are drupes.

Extension shoot, another word for leader, is the one selected to extend the branch, rather than be pruned to form a spur.

Eye describes a growth bud, particularly in grafting and budding. It is also the part of a flower retained by an apple or pear at the end opposite the stalk.

Feathers are the lateral growths on a one-year (maiden) tree.

Fruit buds are larger and fatter than growth buds and develop into flowers and, if pollinated, into fruit.

Grease bands are impregnated sticky papers wrapped around trunks of fruit trees in autumn. These trap wingless females of certain moths as they climb up to lay their eggs.

Heading-back is the winter pruning of the stem of a maiden tree, or older straight-stemmed 'whip', to make it form laterals.

June drop, sometimes extended into July, is when fruitlets drop inexplicably. Possible causes are poor pollination, drought, sudden temperature changes, or natural thinning of an over-crop.

King fruits are those formed by the middle flowers of trusses. Usually larger and with swollen stalks, they can push off the others as they swell and are best removed.

Laterals are side growths at an angle from the main stem. The wider the angle, the stronger the union.

Maiden means a young tree in its first season following grafting or budding.

Mother trees are selected and cared for exclusively for the production of propagation material.

Open-pollinated describes a flower that has been fertilized by pollen from an unknown source.

Pomes are fruits such as apples, pears, medlars, and quinces that have a number of seed-containing cells within a fleshy exterior.

Pomology is the science and practice of fruit growing, a treatise on which is a pomona. Pomona was the Roman goddess of orchards.

Russet is a brown layer of rough skin, almost wholly covering a fruit, as in 'Egremont Russet'.

Scion is the shoot or single bud taken from the mother tree when propagating by grafting or budding on to a rootstock.

Self-fertile, sometimes 'self-compatible', means that the tree can produce seed when fertilized with its own pollen. Self-sterile means that it cannot.

Sport, sometimes 'mutant', is a plant that differs genetically from the typical growth of its parent – it might bear, for instance, fruit with different skin colouring.

Top-worked describes a tree grafted or budded at the top of a rootstock, rather than near the ground.

Triploids. See under Diploids.

Truss is a cluster of flowers or fruit emanating from one bud.

Union is the junction of scion and rootstock on a grafted tree. It shows on the stem of the plant as a swelling, which must be kept above ground level to prevent scion rooting.

Water shoots are vigorous, sappy growths, useless for fruit production, arising from the trunk in the middle of the tree.

Winter wash is tar-oil applied to fruit trees after leaf-fall to clean off lichen and kill over-wintering insects or eggs.

BIBLIOGRAPHY

Baker, Harry, *The Fruit Garden Displayed*, Cassell, 1986

Baker, Harry, *Fruit*, Mitchell Beazley, 1980

Brickell, Christopher, *Pruning*, Mitchell Beazley, 1979

Buczacki, Stefan, *Beat Garden Pests and Diseases*, Penguin, 1985

Bultitude, John, *Apples*, Macmillan, 1983

Bunyard, Edward, *The Anatomy of Dessert*, Dulaw, 1929

Bunyard, Edward, *A Handbook of Hardy Fruits (Apples and Pears)*, John Murray, 1920

Bush, Raymond, *Fruit Growing Outdoors*, Faber & Faber, 1946

Carlson, R. F., *et al.*, *North American Apples: Varieties, Rootstocks, Outlook*, Michigan State University Press, 1970

Gourley, M. S., *Textbook of Pomology*, Macmillan, New York, 1922

Grubb, Norman, *Cherries*, Crosby Lockwood, 1949

Hadfield, Miles, *A History of British Gardening*, Penguin, 1985

Hall, A. D., and Crane, M. B., *The Apple*, Hopkinson, 1933

Harvey, John, *Early Nurserymen*, Phillimore, 1974

Hedrick, Ulysses, *History of Horticulture in America*, Oxford University Press, 1950

Hellyer, A. G. L., *Garden Pest Control*, Collingridge, 1944

Huxley, Anthony, *Penguin Encyclopedia of Gardening*, Allen Lane, 1981

Hyams, Edward, and Jackson, A. A., (eds.), *The Orchard and Fruit Garden*, Longmans, 1961

Johns, Leslie, and Stevenson, Violet, *Fruit for the Home and Garden*, Angus & Robertson, 1985

Ministry of Agriculture (National Fruit Trials), *Indexes of the Apple, Cherry, Pear and Plum Collections*

Ministry of Agriculture (National Fruit Trials), *Catalogue of British Pears*

Ortho Books, *Fruits, Berries and Nuts*, Chevron, 1987

Roach, F. A., *Cultivated Fruits of Britain*, Blackwell, 1985

Royal Horticultural Society, *Fruit Pests, Diseases & Disorders* (Wisley Handbook 27), Cassell, 1980

Royal Horticultural Society, *The Wisley Book of Gardening*, Collingridge, 1981

Simmonds, A., *A Horticultural Who was Who*, Royal Horticultural Society, 1948

Smith, Muriel, *The National Apple Register of the U.K.*, Ministry of Agriculture, 1971

Sunset Books, *Fruits, Nuts and Berries*, Lane, 1984

Taylor, H. V., *The Apples of England*, Crosby Lockwood, 1947

Taylor, H. V., *The Plums of England*, Crosby Lockwood, 1949

Upshall, W. H., (ed.), *History of Fruit Growing and Handling in USA and Canada*, American Pomological Society, 1976

INDEX

ACKNOWLEDGEMENTS

My thanks are due to a number of fruit growers, friendly people all, who have never been sparing of their advice and knowledge whenever I have consulted them, especially during the preparation of this book.

Harry Baker, the Fruit Officer of the Royal Horticultural Society and Deputy Director of their Wisley Garden, Surrey; Dr Frank Alston, Brian Self, and Ken Tobutt at the Institute of Horticultural Research, East Malling, Kent; David Pennell and Dr Andrew Reynolds at the National Fruit Trials, Faversham, Kent; and Dr and Mrs Loren D. Tukey of the American Pomological Society – all have given generously of their time and experience and to them I acknowledge a debt of gratitude.

Andrew and Nick Dunn of Frank P. Matthews Ltd, Tenbury Wells, Worcestershire, and Gillian Suddaby of Matthews Fruit Trees Ltd, Bury St. Edmunds, Suffolk, who continues the work of her late father, Jack Matthews, with whom I co-operated over so many years, are all leading fruit-tree growers; I am ever grateful for the friendly help both these families have always given me.

I owe thanks, too, to Richard Pennell, Anthony Roger, John Laxton, and Margaret Peeters (née Rivers), whose family nurseries have contributed so much to fruit growing over many generations and who also have helped me with this book.

Librarians are most helpful people and those at the R.H.S. Lindley Library, London, the Long Ashton Research Station, and the Gloucestershire County Libraries, Gloucester and Cheltenham, have proved no exception during my researching and I thank them, as well as Brian Frith at the Gloucestershire Records Office.

I am most grateful to Christopher Brickell, Director General of the Royal Horticultural Society, for permission to use the Society's flowering tables of apples, cherries, pears, and plums, up-dated for me by Harry Baker; also to the Controller of H.M. Stationery Office for permission to reprint their Identification Tables of Apples by Groups, as used at the National Fruit Trials and up-dated by Dr Andrew Reynolds for this book.

My biggest debt of all I owe to Robert Pearson, the gardening correspondent of the *Sunday Telegraph*, among many other horticultural commitments. He is a good friend of long standing who has read my copy and corrected a number of inaccuracies (although any that remain are entirely my own responsibility) and has so kindly written the Foreword.

PICTURE CREDITS